Specter's

What Not to Do

PORTUGAL

A Unique Travel Guide

Plan your travel with expert advice and Insider Tips: Travel
confidently, Avoid Common Mistakes, and indulge in Art, Culture,
History, Food, and nature.

Sarah Brekenridge

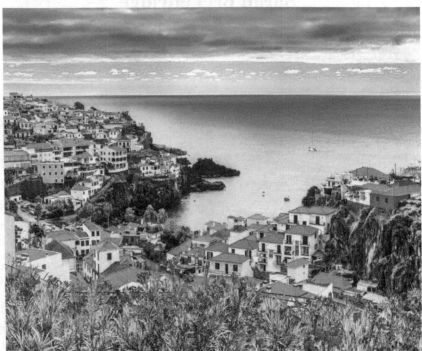

Table of Contents

Introduction

Has there ever been a moment when you unexpectedly encountered a charming bookstore or a picturesque street that wasn't on your map? If you have, you know it felt like you stepped into a secret world. Visiting Portugal is full of hidden gems tucked away from the unusual tourist routes. However, trying to get through the mainstream travel recommendations while planning your trip can pose obstacles and challenges.

It can feel daunting to distinguish between authentic Portuguese experiences and overly commercialized tourist traps, which often need more cultural depth and authenticity. This can impact your desire to immerse yourself in Portuguese culture and history. Once you have an idea of some places you'd like to see and visit, you face budgeting concerns and how to ensure you stay within the budget for your trip. You may also realize other concerns, such as the best ways to get around the country and overcome the language barrier.

Traveling doesn't need to be overwhelming. It is an exciting adventure to visit another country, learn about its rich history, and see stunning architecture. Portugal is a beautiful and charming country with loads to see and do. It's also one of the most romantic countries because of its charming streets and cities. Planning your trip to Portugal is only the start of your adventure, and this book will help guide you through what you should do and avoid while on your journey.

Throughout this book, you can expect a comprehensive guide to preparing you for your trip. You'll learn the planning basics and different ways to get around Portugal. From there, we will dive into the various Portuguese cities to visit. It may feel overwhelming initially, but when you learn what to see and do, you can pave a clear path to experiencing Portugal as authentically as possible while steering yourself away from common pitfalls that could overshadow your trip. Additionally, you will learn the necessary information to discover the hidden gems of Portugal that are often overlooked and some romantic ideas for you and your partner.

Portugal is steeped in rich history, stunning architecture, and a vibrant culture. There is much to discover. Allow this book to inspire you so that when you return home, you have plenty of exciting tales to tell to friends and family about what you got to see and do while in this beautiful European city.

Chapter 1:

Before You Go – Essential Preparation

Did you know that Portugal is one of the sunniest places in Europe? Thanks to its geographical location, the Iberian Peninsula, Portugal sees about 300 days of sunshine. Additionally, Portugal is the place to go if you want to experience some of the liveliest festivals in Europe. The secret to getting the most out of your trip to Portugal starts with when you visit and how well you have prepared. Let's make your trip not just a visit but an adventure into Portugal's rich culture, stunning landscapes, and the welcoming atmosphere of those living there.

Best Time to Visit Portugal

Even though Portugal is not along the Mediterranean, it does experience a Mediterranean climate, which means you can expect hot, dry summers and mild, wet winters (or snow, depending on where in the country you are). This means that deciding to visit Portugal will depend on what you prefer weather-wise. Here is what you can expect in each season:

Spring: Springtime in Portugal will transition from cooler, wetter winter conditions to warmer and drier weather, with the temperature starting to climb to around 68 °F. But don't expect to be basking in sunshine daily, especially in March and April, as this transition can still bring plenty of rain and gray skies. However, as spring progresses, the rainfall will decrease for the most part, though you may still see the odd shower in the northern part of the country. The countryside will blossom with vibrant and colorful flowers dotting the landscape thanks to the rain. Along Portugal's peninsula, May will begin the beach season as the warmer weather starts to roll in around June, and the water temperatures become favorable for swimming.

Summer: By the time summer arrives in June, Portugal will have become pretty hot, perfect for beach days! Temperatures often soar above 86 °F, sometimes higher depending on where you are in the country. Along the coast, you'll find the breeze from the ocean, which will provide some relief, but if you're not great with hot weather, it won't be pleasant to do other outdoor activities besides being at the beach. Summer is also peak tourist season, so flights and accommodations are a little more expensive.

Autumn: Autumn in Portugal will bring milder temperatures back to the country, making it more comfortable for outdoor excursions (temperatures are usually in the 70s during the day and 60s in the evening). Tourist season also starts to wind down, so it won't be as crowded when you visit different attractions around the country. Additionally, autumn marks the start of harvest season, offering opportunities to attend festivals celebrating wine and other produce.

Winter: Winter will vary depending on where you are in the country. Winter tends to be mild, with cooler temperatures and more rain than other seasons. The temperatures typically range between 46 °F and 61 °F, but they can drop lower the further north you go. However, some areas, such as Serra da Estrela, also get snow. Either way, make sure to bring a warm jacket (preferably something that is waterproof) as well as an umbrella.

Key Festivals in Portugal

Portugal is well-known for its cultural celebrations, and a trip would not be complete without immersing yourself in at least one of its many cultural events throughout the year. This list is a high-level overview of the events to check out depending on when you're going to travel to Portugal:

Carnival: Portugal's version of Carnival takes place in February or March. This historical festival has been celebrated since the 16th century to mark the beginning of Lent. Celebrated with vibrancy, Carnival will entertain festivalgoers with parades, street parties, live music, and food.

Holy Week: Holy Week, known as Semana Santa, is another religious observance leading to Easter. Throughout Portugal, cities organize their own unique celebrations. However, the more famous festivities of Holy Week take place in Braga, where the city center is adorned with beautiful flowers. Loulé in the Algarve is also worth visiting during Holy Week, as it hosts large-scale parades.

Fatima Pilgrimage: The Fatima Pilgrimage takes place in May and is of significant cultural and religious importance. This celebration commemorates the apparitions of the Virgin Mary to three young children in May 1917. Annually, on May 13, thousands of pilgrims will gather at the Sanctuary of Our Lady Fatima to pay homage and seek blessings.

Sintra Festival: The Sintra Festival celebrates music and the arts. It is held in the historic town of Sintra, a United Nations Educational, Scientific and Cultural Organization (UNESCO) site, and it brings together ballet dancers, musicians, and pianists to showcase their talents.

Festival of Sardines: The Festival of Sardines, also known as the Santo António Festival or Fest of Saint Anthony, is one of the most popular and lively celebrations, particularly in Lisbon. This celebration is held annually on June 13 to commemorate Saint Anthony of Padua, famous for being the saint of love, marriage, and lost things in Catholicism. This event combines several different celebration methods, including processions of colorful costumes and floats, dancers, and musicians parading their way through the streets. Additionally, there will be food vendors selling grilled sardines to enjoy.

Festa de São João do Porto: The Festa de São João do Porto is an annual celebration held on June 23 in Porto to honor Saint John the Baptist. Interestingly, this festival has pagan routes, but the Christians adopted the traditions. Families celebrating this day will begin their day by eating a meal together. As a visitor, you can enjoy free concerts throughout the day and a fireworks show in the evening.

Portugal Airports and Flying Essentials

Portugal has five major international airports you can fly into depending on where you want to begin your Portuguese adventure. Lisbon Portela Airport (LIS) is situated in the capital city of Lisbon and is the main gateway into Portugal. If you plan to start in Porto, you'll fly into Francisco Sá Carneiro Airport (OPO). This airport also serves as an airport that can connect you to other parts of Europe. If you want to go and enjoy the coastal side of Portugal, you'll be flying into Faro Airport (FAO) in the Algarve region. On the other hand, if you want to explore Madeira Island, you'll fly into Madeira Airport (FNC), and to go to the Azores, you'll need to fly into João Paulo II Airport (PDL).

As you begin to research your flights, one of the best ways to get the best deals is by putting on an alert to find the different prices. Also, it's always useful to be flexible on when you want to travel. Some days are more expensive to fly than others, so if you're okay with flying on a Wednesday or Thursday, you can save some money there. Try to book your flights at least three months in advance to get the best prices available. Remember that if you're planning to visit during peak season, flights will be more expensive than the off-season times of traveling to the country.

Travel Insurance

As you book your flights, one thing that will pop up is travel insurance and if you should purchase it. It's always a wise investment to protect yourself because life can happen. As you choose travel insurance, here is what you should be looking for:

- What the coverage options are, including medical expenses, lost baggage, trip interruption, cancellation, or delays
- What are the limits for your travel policy, including if you have any existing medical conditions and what wouldn't be covered by the policy
- Medical coverage if you get injured or fall ill and require medical assistance
- What travel assistance services are included in the policy? Ideally, you want 24/7 travel assistance services

Visa and Other Documentation

For US citizens, your passport is the only documentation you need unless you plan to stay in Portugal for over 90 days. Double-check when it expires, as it should be valid for at least 90 days beyond your departure date from Portugal to return home to the US or Canada.

Should you need the U.S. Embassy or Consulate, they can be found in Lisbon and Ponta Delgada:

- **U.S. Embassy Lisbon:** Av. das Forças Armadas, Sete-Rios 1600-081 Lisbon
- **U.S. Consulate Ponta Delgada:** Av. Príncipe do Mónaco No, 6-2 F 9500-237 Ponta Delgada, Açores

Packing Essentials for Portugal

The next predicament in preparing for your Portuguese trip is what to pack. One of the best things you can do when it comes to actually packing for your trip is to look at the weather ahead of time. Most weather apps can forecast up to 14 days, which is a good starting point. If you're going to Portugal between March and May, you'll want warmer clothes, a rain jacket, and waterproof shoes. On the other hand, if you'll be traveling to Portugal in July, you'll want to bring a swimsuit.

A helpful tip is to use packable cubes that compress to save room in your bag. When you pack those packable cubes, try to pick outfits you can mix and match over the first few days, and in the next packable cube, pack the next set of clothes you plan to wear. Use this list as a starting point:

- lightweight, breathable tops and T-shirts
- shorts or a skirt for warmer weather
- light sweater or jacket for cooler evenings, especially if you are traveling in spring or autumn
- comfortable walking shoes
- sandals for beach outings
- swimsuit
- hat and sunglasses
- umbrella or lightweight rain jacket, especially if you are going to Portugal in the fall or winter
- sunscreen
- a power adapter to fit Portuguese electrical outlets
- portable charger
- travel-sized toiletries
- travel towel for the beach (or watching the sunset at the beach)

In addition to things to pack, it is also worth purchasing an eSIM for your phone to stay connected without getting hit with massive roaming fees. HolaFly is an excellent company that offers this service; eSIMs from HolaFly can be purchased for trips up to 90 days.

Currency in Portugal

As Portugal is a part of Europe, their currency is the euro (€). Carrying cash with you is always wise, though most hotels, restaurants, and attractions accept MasterCard and Visa. If you plan to bring some euros with you, buy currency before you leave for your trip, either through your bank or through a currency exchange store such as Currency Exchange International. Traveler tip: If you wait to buy euros until you are at the airport in Portugal or at home, you'll likely encounter paying higher exchange fees, so it's best to avoid exchanging currency there. You can also check with your credit card provider to see their exchange rates if you plan to use your credit card for most transactions.

Another handy way to save money is to get a Wise card. This convenient card will give you the best rate and you can easily top it up on their app. You should also pick up a Lisbon Card, which can be purchased through GetYourGuide and will save you money on various attractions if you are planning to visit Lisbon. This card starts at €22 for adults and €15 for children for a 24-hour pass.

Understanding Portuguese Etiquette

As a visitor to Portugal, you will face different ways of living and socializing around one another compared to what you are used to back home. Therefore, you must be mindful of Portuguese etiquette to respect their culture. One of the key aspects, especially if you are staying at a bed and breakfast, is to shake the hands of the person who is hosting you and address them by *Senhor* (Mr.) or *Senjora* (Mrs.) and their last name, unless you have been invited to use their first time. Also, remember to wipe your shoes on the mat before you step inside. Additionally, if your host offers you a refreshment, don't decline, as it can be seen as impolite.

When you eat out at a restaurant, tipping is appreciated but not obligatory unless you are in an area that sees plenty of tourist activity if you tip, round the bill up by 10 to 15%.

It is considered rude if you plan to visit churches while mass is ongoing. If you decide to join the mass, don't take photos, as they will distract other churchgoers. Also, be mindful that if you visit churches or other sacred sites, you may be required to wear modest attire.

Lastly, try to speak Portuguese as often as possible rather than Spanish. While the languages are similar, some may view this as poor etiquette. Google Translate or Apple's translation app will be helpful when you are trying to overcome the language barrier. However, if you want to start practicing now, try out Duolingo to help you master some basic Portuguese phrases.

Planning a Romantic Holiday to Portugal

If you happen to be planning your trip to Portugal as a romantic getaway or honeymoon, you should try to incorporate some romantic things to do while on your vacation. Plenty of spots throughout the country paint the perfect romantic setting, including beaches where you can watch the sunset or lively city centers where you can enjoy a romantic night out. Plenty of accommodations will enhance your romantic experience, including charming *quintas* in the countryside and boutique hotels. We will cover accommodation options, some of which will help with your romantic holiday planning. Other things you can consider doing include wine-tasting tours, couples spa day in Sintra, a hot air balloon ride over the Alentejo countryside, sunset cruises, especially along the Douro River in Porto, and romantic strolls through the Alfama district in Lisbon, etc.

These are just some ideas that spark a little imagination. Of course, as we explore the different regions of Portugal, we will look at some romantic ideas to make your trip unforgettable with your partner!

What Not to Do While Planning Your Portuguese Adventure

Don't Pack High Heels

Portugal has a lot of cobbled streets! While you may want to look fancy on a night out, there is no point in risking injuring your ankle. Opt for wedges or cute flats that will be easier to walk around in if you're going to have a nice night out.

Don't Have Lunch before 1 pm and Dinner before 7 pm.

Lunch and dinner are sacred times of the day for any Portuguese citizen, often starting later than you might be used to. In Portugal, most restaurants serve lunch beginning around 1 p.m., with service continuing until 3 p.m. Similarly, dinners typically start around 7 or 8 p.m. and can last until 11 p.m. However, it's important to note that there are exceptions and varying opening and closing hours depending on the restaurant. Please check with restaurants on timings before heading to lunch or dinner.

Don't Tip Excessively

Tipping is not mandatory in Portugal. Tipping is seen as a generous act of recognizing exceptionally good service. Either way, waiters will give you the best of the service without expecting this "reward."

Always Carry Sunscreen

Portugal is renowned for its beautiful weather, and you will end up spending most of your time outdoors. With sun-soaked skies and sandy beaches, staying indoors is hard to imagine. When visiting Portugal, you'll likely want to enjoy blissful days on the Algarve's beaches or stroll around Lisbon's charming streets. However, in either location, the sun can be your enemy, so you must be prepared to protect yourself. It's advisable to carry sunscreen whenever you are visiting open spaces with lots of sunlight.

Portugal is not Spain

Spain and Portugal are neighboring countries, but Portugal is often mistaken for Spain. Despite its smaller size, many people confuse Portugal with its neighbor. This mix-up can be frustrating for the local Portuguese! The reason is simple: visiting Portugal and then Spain reveals many distinct cultural differences between the two countries.

What one should avoid is speaking in Spanish in Portugal. While Portuguese might initially sound similar to Spanish, but it's quite different! When visiting Portugal, you'll find that most Portuguese people are more comfortable speaking English with you than Spanish.

Don't Start Arguments on Football

Football is like a sacred religion to the Portuguese people! The sport gained popularity as early as the 19th century. It won't be an exaggeration to say that Portuguese people live and breathe football. Football is very close to the heart and arouses strong emotions in the fans. So, you can share your praises, talk about players, and demonstrate your liking for football. However, do not express your liking for a specific club or team. That may start an unnecessary discussion with locals.

Learning to Navigate Portugal

Planning your trip to Portugal is just the beginning of your adventure. When you have packed your bags, etiquette in check, and romantic plans ready, you're just about ready to explore Portugal. However, navigating this beautiful European city confidently will require more planning and learning before your plane departs from home and touches down in Portugal. In the next chapter, we will explore how to get around Portugal, exploring the best transportation options to get you from one place to the next. We will also cover some romantic routes to follow.

Chapter 2:

Navigating Portugal – Transportation Tips

H ave you ever imagined sailing down the Douro River at sunset or driving through the picturesque hills around Sintra with your partner? Portugal has many diverse landscapes, each with charm and beauty. Finding your way around the country will offer limitless opportunities to see the many different sites. There are many ways to get around the country, so which is best for you? This chapter will cover all the various ways to travel around Portugal to help you decide the best way for you.

How to Get Around Portugal

The nice thing about Portugal is that it is a small country, so you can easily get around by train, bus, and public transportation, which is perfect if you don't want to drive. Of course, with a car, you have more flexibility with getting to hidden gems or not being stuck to a strict timeline, especially with trains and buses. However you decide to get around, whether it's a mix of transportation modes or sticking to one, you'll be able to take in the scenic sites of the country while going from one point to the next.

By Train

One of the best ways to get around Portugal is by train. The train offers a scenic way to see the country's landscapes without the stress of navigating the roads. Portugal has a well-established rail network operated by Comboios de Portugal (CP), which allows you to take short and long distances throughout the country. You will find more picturesque lines in northern Portugal, especially if you take the train between Porto and Pocinho. Some other things to keep in mind when you book your tickets online are the following codes:

- **Regional (R):** Hopping on a regional train is the slower option, as it stops at nearly every station along its designated route.
- **Interregional (IR):** These trains are slightly faster than the regional and skip the smaller stations along their designated routes.
- **Intercidades (IC):** These express trains stop in major cities only. You must reserve your seats if you take an IC train.
- **Alfa Pendular Deluxe (AP):** This option is faster than taking the express trains. However, tickets for this train are pricey. If you take the AP train, you must reserve your seats.

By Public Transportation

Lisbon and Porto have metro and public buses to get you around their beautiful cities.

Metro in Lisbon

Lisbon has four metro lines that are easy to follow and are all marked with different colors. There are also buses to get you around as you need, too. When using Lisbon's metro system, the fare is €1.80 and can be paid with a contactless bank card (such as a credit card, Apple Pay, or Google Pay). You can also purchase a rechargeable "Navegante" card. These cards also work on the buses, trams, and ferries. Your other option is to pick up a 24-hour pass that will give you access to the metro, buses, Carris (trams), and their CP trains, which range from €6.80 to €10.80. If you are taking a public bus, remember to wave the bus down so it doesn't drive by you!

In addition to the metro and buses, Lisbon has a tram service, but don't confuse the yellow ones with the red ones! The red ones are a hop-on, hop-off tourist option, and the day passes, or your contactless payment won't work on them. Of the six yellow tram lines, the most popular line to follow is vintage tram 28, which will take you through the older part of the city with plenty of scenic views.

As for the Commuter Train System called "CP," four lines will bring you to the outer parts of Lisbon. The Sintra and Cascais lines will bring you to various tourist attractions and help you catch the ferry to Tróia Peninsula. Otherwise, the other lines are Azambuja and Sado.

Metro in Porto

The metro system in Porto, called Metro do Porto, is also easy to follow and has six lines to connect you to various neighborhoods, suburbs, and other points of interest in the city. The metro lines are labeled A through F and have distinct colors to make determining what line you need to take easier. Porto also has public buses to get you around the city or the greater Porto area.

To board the metro and buses in Porto, you must pick up an "Andante" card, which is available at the stations and the airport. It is €0.50 to buy. Each journey is €1.40 for the metro and €1.85 for the buses. If you top your card up with ten journeys, you will get one for free. Alternatively, you can pick up an Andante 24, which will give you unlimited travel for 24 hours to bring you through the different zones. Be sure to double-check, as the zone prices range between €5.15 and €16.70 and are only valid in the zone the ticket specifies.

Remember to utilize Google Maps, which can help you determine which method of public transportation is best for your destination in and around Lisbon and Porto.

By Rental Car

Renting a car is one of the most convenient ways to travel at your leisure. If you plan to rent a car in Portugal, you must have a valid driver's license and be at least 18 years old. You should also purchase rental car insurance to protect yourself against accidents or car theft. When you pick up your car, it is wise to do a video while inspecting it for any previous scratches or dents.

Portugal drives on the right side of the road. If you rent a car, familiarize yourself with their road laws, including speed limits, traffic signs, and the right-of-way rules. For example, the speed limits in Portugal are between 32 miles per hour (50 kilometers per hour or kph) and 55 mph (99 kph), and on motorways, it is 74 mph (120 kph). Be mindful of your speed and always pay attention to signs that post the speed limit. When you come to an intersection, vehicles from your right will always have the right of way. Pedestrians also have the right of way at a marked or unmarked crosswalk. Also, Portugal has plenty of roundabouts, so familiarize yourself with navigating these.

Some other things to note about driving in Portugal are that many motorways have toll roads, where you will need to pay a fee at the toll gate. Ensure you use the lanes with a green light above them and not the lane that says "Via Verde," as that is an automatic debit-payment lane. The lanes with the green lights allow you to pay the toll with cash or by Visa or MasterCard.

By Bus

Exploring Portugal by bus will offer an affordable and flexible way to navigate the country without the stress of driving. One of Portugal's national bus service companies that offers frequent service to various cities is the Rede Expressos. However, the other bus operators you will come across are

- Rodonorte
- Rodoviária do Alentejo
- Rodotejo
- Eva
- Frota Azul

Most bus ticket companies offer online booking services, but you can also buy them at bus stations. If you're traveling during peak season, try to book your tickets early enough to ensure you can get on the bus when you want. Most bus tickets are relatively affordable, some as low as €20 depending on the distance between the cities. Children under four get to travel free, while kids between 5 and 13 get half the price of an adult ticket. There are also discounts for travelers under 29 and seniors who are 65 and up.

By Taxi

Getting a taxi is one of the more expensive ways to get around Portugal, but it is also convenient to take your luggage to your accommodations or a train or bus station in the more rural towns. You can hail a taxi from designated taxi stands or through an app. Ensure taxi meters are running or agree on a fare before you begin your journey.

Ordering an Uber is also an option. Just be sure to change your location!

By Bicycle

Renting a bicycle to see the coastal towns is a great way to take in the sights, especially if you want to explore some areas off the beaten path. Some hotels offer bike-for-hire services. However, options are also available if you and your partner want to take a bike tour. One of the top companies to check out for bike tour purposes is Top Bike Tours Portugal.

Romantic Routes Unveiled

If you are going to Portugal with romance in mind, whether to pop the question or go on a honeymoon or an anniversary trip, it is always worth planning some romantic routes. Driving is one way to do this if you rent a car. Otherwise, there are some great scenic train journeys you can follow, too.

Driving Through Alentejo

Driving through the serene landscape of cork oak forests and vineyards in Alentejo is a peaceful way to adventure with your loved one and explore this part of Portugal without an agenda. You may want to visit some wineries and taste delicious Portuguese wines. The top wineries include

- Adega Mayor
- Herdade do Esporao
- Entouismo Cartuxa
- Fitapreta Vinhos
- Ravasqueira

On your trip, it's also worth exploring some of the quaint towns. Put these on your road trip bucket list if you are driving through Alentejo:

- **Mértola:** Mértola is in the south part of the Alentejo region, overlooking the Guadiana River. This quaint town has plenty of medieval and Moorish history to unfold. This beautiful town has lovely, narrow, cobblestoned streets with wrought-iron balconies overlooking them, making you feel like you've stepped back in time.
- **Vila Nova de Milfontes:** Vila Nova de Milfontes is a picturesque coastal town along Aletenjo's coastline. This town is known for its beautiful beaches and is lively at night, especially in the summer!
- **Zambujeira do Mar:** Zambujeira do Mar is a cute seaside town along Altenjo's coastline. Like Vila Nova de Milfontes, it boasts beautiful beaches and crystal-clear waters. Visiting this small town is great if you and your partner are adventuring and love to hike or enjoy other outdoor activities.

Taking the Train to Sintra

Sintra is an easy place to go for a day trip while in Lisbon, and taking the train is one of the most romantic (and cost-efficient ways to do this). This short 40-minute train ride will take you along a picturesque route to the small town, with beautiful landscapes, lush forests, and clouds hanging above the distant mountaintops along the way. It's as dreamy as it sounds.

When you arrive in Sintra, plenty of romance will be had with the many gardens and palaces. Some of the top romantic spots to visit in Sintra include

- Quinta da Regaleira
- Castelo dos Mouros
- the National Palace of Pena
- Praia da Ursa

Take the time to explore with your partner, taking in as many sights as possible. Then, board the train to return to Lisbon after the sun has set.

Driving the Coastal Routes

You can follow many coastal routes in Portugal, which will take you to many romantic spots in the country. If you're looking for some road trip ideas, here are some of the top drives:

- **Lisbon, Cascais, and Sintra:** Starting in Lisbon, follow the roads that will bring you along the scenic Estrada Marginal, which hugs Portugal's coastline and offers panoramic views of the sandy beaches and cliffs. Along the way, you'll come across Cascais, a charming seaside town with lovely buildings and a beautiful harbor. This is a great place to grab lunch and stroll along the promenade. When you are ready to head back on the road to Sintra, stop by Guincho Beach, famous for its great surf. From there, head inland to Sintra, where the romantic spots will continue with the gardens and palaces. The National Palace of Pena, perched atop a hilltop with panoramic coastline views, is worth exploring.
- **Albufeira to Sagres:** The coastal journey from Albufeira to Sagres is one of the best ways to view the rugged cliffs of the Algarve. This road trip follows the N125 road westward, passing charming fishing villages and hidden coves along the way. Make a stop at the Praia da Marinha, famous for its limestone cliffs and crystal-clear waters, perfect for a refreshing swim. As you continue to Sagres, the landscapes become more beautiful, with windswept cliffs plunging into the Atlantic Ocean below. Once you arrive in Sagres, visit Cape St. Vincent for the panoramic views.
- **Drive around São Miguel Island in the Azores:** It is one of the most scenic and beautiful drives you and your love can follow, where you can see dramatic cliffs, volcanic landscapes, stunning views of the Atlantic Ocean, and flower meadows around every turn. For this drive, you will want to start in Ponta Delgada and follow the coastal road as it loops you around São Miguel Island. As you drive, stop in Sete Cidades, a picturesque village famous for its lush greenery and the twin lakes of Lagoa Azul and Lagoa Verde set in the crater of a dormant volcano. Continue your journey to the thermal springs in

the Furnas Valley, where you can soak in different pools that are believed to have healing properties. If you return to Ponta Delgada in time, you can catch the sunset over the harbor.

Where to Stop for Stunning Views

The best times to take coastal road trips through Portugal's Algarve and Atlantic Road vary depending on your preferences and the weather conditions. For example, the weather will be perfect if you go to the Algarve between June and August. Still, because it will coincide with peak season, you can expect more crowds, therefore making it more challenging to find parking in many places. Alternatively, if you want to avoid the crowds and make the most of your road trip, you may want to plan your trip in April, May, September, or October, guaranteeing pleasant weather and temperatures. For the Atlantic Road, especially if you drive from Porto to Caminha, spring and fall bring milder weather, which is ideal for taking in the coastal scenery without the increase of fellow tourists.

As for stopping for unforgettable views, some iconic spots are the Praia de Marinha, famous for the limestone formations in the turquoise waters, or the Ponta da Piedade near Lagos for breathtaking coastal vistas. If you want to take in the landscape from one of the highest points, you will want to hike the Fóia in Monchique, where the summit will give you unparalleled coastline views. For other great views and appreciating architecture, towns like Viana do Castelo and Caminha are great places to pop into and explore. They also offer great coastal views with their unique perspectives.

Surprise your partner at lesser-known beaches or viewpoints to make the trip extra special. If you can time your visits, there are plenty of areas to catch the sunset and various scenic spots, like Carvoeiro Beach. You may even want to surprise your partner by taking them to a wine-tasting session or pack a picnic lunch with delicacies from local stores while taking in the scenery at a scenic outlook or secluded beach.

Whatever you decide to add a little romance to your journey, there are plenty of ways to do it, whether spontaneous or not. The scenery of Portugal is already romantic with its vast landscapes, so finding the right ways to spend time together will be a thrilling adventure.

Staying Safe in Portugal

As with anywhere you go, even in your hometown, exercising caution and being aware of your surroundings is always best. That said, Portugal is a safe country to visit. The only one of the more significant concerns in this country is petty theft and pickpocketing. The common sense advice to avoid becoming a victim of such crimes is to keep your belongings in sight and secure at all times, ensuring you don't keep your wallet or phone in an outer pocket that would otherwise be easy to steal. Avoid bringing anything nonessential with you and keep it locked in a safe, such as your passport.

As for scams, there will always be someone who will try to grab your attention and scam you. Here are some scams to keep an eye out for:

The rosemary scam: In this scam, an older woman approaches you, offering a sprig of rosemary. Before you can decline it, she grabs your hand and starts telling your fortune. She demands you pay her for her services when she's done. If you don't pay her, she will make a scene until you give her what she wants. If someone does approach you and tries to grab your hand, the most effective response is to retract your hand quickly and walk away.

The petition scam: If someone approaches you with a petition, say, "não, Obrigado," which means "no, thank you," and walk away. This is a way to distract you so the person's accomplices can pickpocket.

The slip-and-fall scam: This scam often happens on public transportation where someone will purposely slip or trip into you. This contact makes it easy for the person to pickpocket by distracting you. When you are on public transportation, always keep your belongings close and secure to you. If this happens, check your belongings immediately.

Emergency Numbers and U.S. Embassy

Should you ever need to call the police or other emergency services in Portugal, the number to dial is 112.

If you need U.S. Services while on your trip, the embassy is in Lisbon. The address is Avenida das Forças Armadas, 1600-081.

First Stop: Lisbon

Getting around Portugal is easier than you may have thought at the start of this chapter, especially with the country's vast network of trains and buses and public transportation options in Lisbon and Porto. This chapter gave you all the insights you need to make the decisions that will best suit your Portuguese adventure and some beautiful coastal adventures you can take with your love. Additionally, you are now armed with the knowledge of how to stay safe while you adventure through this beautiful European country.

With all of that in mind and checked off, it's time to start exploring what Portugal offers. Our first spot in the country is Lisbon, where we can uncover the various attractions to explore and do other things to make your time in this iconic city memorable.

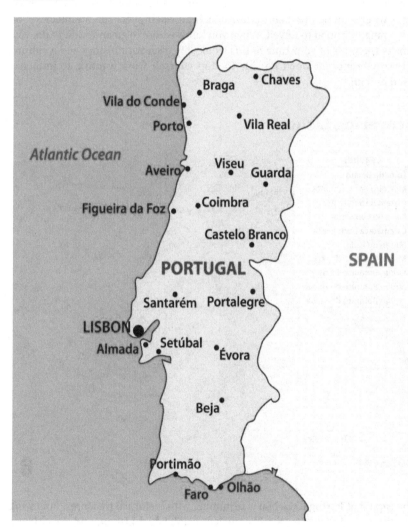

Chapter 3:

Lisbon—Dos and Don'ts

P icture yourself wandering through the cobblestoned streets of Lisbon, where there are many stories behind each piece of architecture or neighborhood to unveil. When you know where to go and what to do, you can make the most of your time in this iconic city, rich with history and a culture that is so vibrant you won't be able to stop yourself from wanting to immerse yourself in it all.

Discovering Lisbon

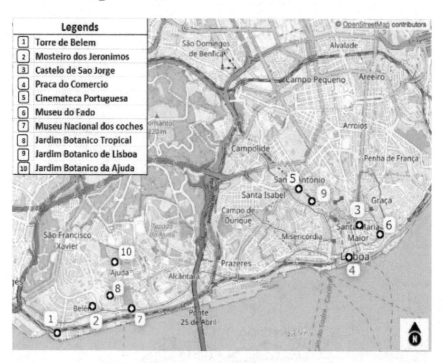

Legends	
1	Torre de Belem
2	Mosteiro dos Jeronimos
3	Castelo de Sao Jorge
4	Praca do Comercio
5	Cinemateca Portuguesa
6	Museu do Fado
7	Museu Nacional dos coches
8	Jardim Botanico Tropical
9	Jardim Botanico de Lisboa
10	Jardim Botanico da Ajuda

As the capital of Portugal, Lisbon is brimming with historical treasures. Following the settlement of the Celts, the Phoenicians established Lisbon, and the city was later inhabited by the Romans in 205, the Moors in 711, and the Christians in 1147. Given the many people who lived in Lisbon before our time, Lisbon's rich heritage is embedded in its diverse architecture, streets, and iconic monuments. Places like the Jerónimos Monastery and São Jorge Castle reflect Lisbon's past, and districts like Alfama offer visitors a glimpse into traditional Portuguese life. And of course, there are plenty of gardens where you can relax and enjoy a picnic throughout the city.

Whatever the reason that is bringing you to this beautiful and vibrant city, use this guide to help you craft an itinerary to make the most of your time in this Portuguese capital city while avoiding common pitfalls that could hinder some of your trips.

What to Do in Lisbon

Torre de Belém

Address: Av. Brasília, 1400-038 Lisbon

Hours of operation

- May to September: 10 a.m. to 6:30 p.m. (the last admission is at 6 p.m.)
- October to April: 10 a.m. to 5:30 p.m. (the last admission is at 5 p.m.)
- Closed on Mondays, January 1, Easter Sunday, May 1, June 13, and Christmas Day

Torre de Belém (Belém Tower) is a United Nations Educational, Scientific, and Cultural (UNESCO) Site along the Tagus River. Built between 1514 and 1520 by the military architect Francisco de Arruda, Belém Tower was a fortress to defend

Lisbon. It transitioned to being a gateway to the city and later served as a lighthouse. At this tower, you can explore and admire the impressive Manueline architecture adorned with carvings and other motifs; check out the interior of the building, including the king's and governor's chambers, audience hall, and chapel; and climb the staircase to the rooftop terrace to take in the panoramic views of the river.

This attraction costs €8 for visitors 13 and up and is free for those 12 and under or those with a Lisbon Card. Additionally, the first Sunday of every month is free.

Mosteiro dos Jerónimos

Address: Praça do Império 1400-206 Lisbon

Hours of operation: 10 a.m. to 6 p.m. daily

Mosteiro dos Jerónimos (Jerónimos Monastery) is another UNESCO World Heritage Site in Lisbon and is another one of Lisbon's most important landmarks. Commissioned by King Manuel I, construction began for the monastery in 1501 but wasn't completed until the 17th century. The significance of this monastery is that it was built on the former site of Ermida do Restelo. Vasco da Gama and other sailors prayed for safety at Ermida do Restelo before embarking on a journey to India along the African Coast.

When you visit Jerónimos Monastery, you'll be able to admire the architecture (most of it is Manueline) and the ornate façade covered with maritime motifs. Inside, the exquisiteness of the monastery continues in its chapel and two-story cloister, where you can see the tomb of Vasco da Gama alongside Portuguese poet and writer Luís de Camões.

The church is free to explore. However, there is an admission for the abbey.

Ticket type	Price
Adults	€ 10
Senior and students	€ 5
Children (12 and under)	Free
Lisbon cardholders	Free

Castelo de São Jorge

Address: R. de Santa Cruz do Castelo, 1100-129 Lisbon

Hours of operation

- November to February: 9 a.m. to 6 p.m.
- March to October: 9 a.m. to 9 p.m.

Perched atop the highest point in Lisbon is the magnificent Castelo de São Jorge (São Jorge Castle), a fifth-century fortress that was built by the Visigoths and enhanced by the Moors in the 11th century. At this castle, you will explore the building, admire the architecture, and immerse yourself in the castle's past. It may take up to four hours to see everything because of the castle's size. It is also worth exploring the rest of the district when you are done at São Jorge Castle, as there is much more architecture to admire along the surrounding streets.

Ticket type	Price
Adults	€ 10
Seniors (65 years old and up)	€ 8.50
Students	€ 5
Children 12 and under	Free

Praça do Comércio

Praça do Comércio, also known as Commerce Square, is one of Lisbon's most significant historical landmarks. It was a crucial area for maritime trade. Originally the site of the Royal Palace, until a devastating earthquake rocked Lisbon in 1775, the square was rebuilt as a symbol of Portugal's resilience and maritime power.

This square looks out to the Tagus River on the southern end and is bordered by elegant yellow buildings adorned with arches.

At this square, you can explore the expansive space, walk along the river's promenade, or enjoy a drink at one of the cafés. Some of the notable highlights of the square are the Equestrian Statue of Joseph I, who was once king of Portugal, and the Rua Augusta Arch, which leads to Baxia Street.

Cinemateca Portuguesa

Address: Rua Barata Salgueiro 39, Lisbon, 1269-059

Cinemateca Portuguesa (Portuguese Cinematheque)is the place for movie buffs, especially those who appreciate old 1940s movie theater architecture. This movie theater serves Portugal's National Film Archive and Cultural Center, which is dedicated to preserving and promoting Portuguese international cinema. Opened to the public in 1948, visiting this movie theater allows you to explore the art of filmmaking with its extensive collection of films (over 21,0000) ranging from classics to contemporary works. In addition to watching movies, this theater has a museum with temporary and permanent exhibitions where you can see rare memorabilia, posters, and old film equipment, including film reels, projectors, and canisters.

For more movie magic, there is a small room to the side of the theater and a museum adorned with a starry sky ceiling. Cinemateca Portuguesa also has a rooftop café and bookshop.

Museu do Fado

Address: Largo do Chafariz de Dentro, N.º 1, 1100-139 Lisboa

Hours of operation: 10 a.m. to 6 p.m. (the last entry is at 5:30 p.m.; closed on Mondays, January 1, May 1 and December 25)

Museu do Fado (The Fado Museum) is a museum in the Alfama District dedicated to celebrating Portugal's musical heritage. This museum pays homage to fado (which translates to fate), a traditional Portuguese music genre renowned for its heartfelt lyrics and beautiful melodies that capture the essence of longing. The museum is housed in a beautifully restored 18th-century building. It will give you an immersive experience as you learn the history and evolution of fado, with memorabilia and artifacts on display, as well as interactive exhibits that will highlight the significance of this music genre in Portuguese culture. You'll also get to see the collection of musical instruments, costumes, and recordings to gain insight into the lives and legacies of some of the fado's iconic performers.

Additionally, Museu do Fado hosts live performances where you can experience the music in an authentic setting. Upcoming performances are listed on their website.

Ticket type	Price
Adults	€ 5
Students (13 to 25 years old)	€ 2.50
Seniors (65 years old and up)	€ 4.30
Lisbon cardholders	€ 4
Children with a Lisbon card	€ 2
Children 12 and under	Free
Guided tour (one hour long)	€3 per person

Museu Nacional dos Coches

Address: Av. da Índia 136, 1300-300 Lisboa

Hours of operation

- Museu Nacional dos Coches (new building): 10 a.m. to 6 p.m. (closed on Mondays)
- Royal Picadeiro: 10 a.m. to 6 p.m. (closed on Tuesdays)
- The last time to enter is at 5:30 p.m. for both museums.

Museu Nacional dos Coches (The National Coach Museum) is fascinating as it displays the history and evolution of royal carriages in Portugal and Europe between the 17th and 19th centuries. The coaches are housed in a newer modern building and the original riding school house (Picadeiro Real or Royal Picadeiro), established in May 1905.

While visiting the museum, you will see the fantastic craftsmanship that went into creating the coaches and learn about the carriages' role in royal ceremonies. In addition to admiring the coaches, you will see several paintings and other artifacts from various centuries. This museum is unique and not one to miss!

Ticket type	Museu Nacional dos Coches	Royal Picadeiro
Adults	€ 8	€ 5
Children (12 years old and under)	Free	Free
Lisbon cardholders	Free	Free

Gardens to Spend Time In

Lisbon has many gardens worth exploring, especially since they are free! This is a great way to escape from the bustling city streets so that you can unwind amidst the trees and flowerbeds and find some relaxation for your trip:

Jardim Botânico Tropical:
Dating back to the early 1900s, the Jardim Botânico Tropical (Tropical Botanical Garden) spans over seventeen acres, showcasing a diverse collection of exotic plants, trees, and flowers from the former Portuguese colonies who lived in Africa and Asia. Visiting this garden lets you enjoy a lovely nature walk in the tranquil atmosphere.

Jardim Botânico de Lisboa:
Tucked behind the Museum of Natural History, the Jardim Botânico de Lisboa (Lisbon Botanical Garden) is a tranquil garden with an extensive collection of plants from around the world, perfectly curated into themed gardens and greenhouses. In this garden, you can wander the winding pathways lined with beautiful flowers, trees, and other exotic plants while enjoying the peaceful ambiance. It's an often forgotten garden, but back in the day, it was one of the best gardens to visit in Europe. It also served as a teaching and research facility for the Polytechnic school in the mid-19th century.

Jardim Botânico da Ajuda:
The Jardim Botânico da Ajuda (Ajuda Botanical Garden) dates back to 1768 when it was built as part of the royal palace of Ajuda. This charming garden is over eight acres and has a diverse collection of plants from around the world, including trees from Portugal's older colonies. This park is a great place to stop by if you want to picnic with your significant other!

Neighborhoods to Explore in Lisbon

Odivelas

Odivelas, located on the outskirts of Lisbon and reachable via the final stop on the yellow metro line, is a hidden gem waiting to be discovered. Steeped in centuries of history, the quaint streets offer you a chance to view Lisbon's past. One of the cultural landmarks worth exploring is the Monastery of São Dinis de Odivelas, a significant landmark dating back to the 14th century and the resting place of King Dinis. It also showcases a blend of architectural styles like Baroque, Gothic, and Manueline. Apart from its historical charm, Odivelas offers the Strada Outlet for shopping enthusiasts, numerous cozy cafés, and family-run eateries serving delectable Portuguese cuisine.

Avenidas Novas

Avenidas Novas is an elegant neighborhood with streets lined by magnificent mansion homes and Art Nouveau buildings. Visiting this neighborhood will allow you to admire the beautiful architecture of these homes and buildings and the Gulbenkian Museum, which houses a collection of art and cultural artifacts. If you walk along Avenida Roma, there will be plenty of shopping opportunities, from boutique clothing stores to bookstores. Avenidas Novas also has plenty of cafés where you can enjoy delicious Portuguese sweets with a coffee or indulge in seafood.

Campo de Ourique

Campo de Ourique is one of the least touristy neighborhoods to explore in Lisbon, making it an ideal way to spend a few hours away from the hustle and bustle of the city center. This neighborhood has beautiful tree-lined streets, cozy cafés, and an overall relaxed atmosphere. If you want to immerse yourself in some of the market life, check out the Mercado de Campo de Ourique, where you can sample delicacies while mingling with locals and shop for authentic Portuguese gifts in the shops.

Madragoa

Madragoa is a less touristy neighborhood situated near the Tagus River. Visiting this hidden gem will offer you a glimpse into the traditional lives of the locals. Wander through the narrow streets lined with colorful tiled houses with classic wrought-iron balconies overlooking the streets. This neighborhood is also known for its thriving art community. As such, you can check out the Museu da Marioneta (Marionette Museum), where thousands of puppets from around the world are on display.

Alcântara

Alcântara was once an industrialized area that helped Lisbon thrive. Today, the old warehouses have been converted into other businesses, art galleries, shops, and a beautiful bookstore. If you visit this hidden neighborhood gem, be sure to stop by the iconic 25 de Abril Bridge to take in the sites of the Tagus River.

Beyond exploring the architecture, one of the best cultural attractions to check out is the LX Factory, a creative hub with shops, studios, restaurants, and cafés.

Romantic Spots in Lisbon

Next to Paris, Lisbon is easily one of the most romantic places to visit in Europe, especially for those traveling on their honeymoon, celebrating an anniversary, or getting engaged. The city has much charm, including the stunning views of the Tagus River and the intimate settings in some historic neighborhoods like Alfama and Bairro Alto, enhancing the romance. Here are some of the romantic spots you can check out to make this trip extra special with your significant other:

Watch the sunset at Miradouro das Portas do Sol.
Miradouro das Portas do Sol, which means "the gate of the sun," is one of the best places to watch the sunrise over Lisbon. This is a beautiful and tranquil way to start your day with your partner before heading to your planned adventures. If you want to make your morning special, head to St. George's Castle for breakfast.

Head to Belém for the sunset.
Lisbon is the only city in Europe where you can watch the sun set into the sea for the night. However, the only place to watch this pretty spectacle is in Belém.

Spend the day in Sintra.
In the last chapter, we covered the romantic train trip you can take to Sintra. However, this town reminds many of a fairytale with its palaces and more.

Have a picnic and eat at Jardim Botânico Tropical.
Since Jardim Botânico Tropical is a tropical paradise in Lisbon, why not pack a picnic while sprawling on the expansive green space? While packing your lunch, don't forget to pick up some delicious Portuguese pastries!

Take a cruise along the Tagus River.
At just over 625 miles long, the Tagus River is the longest in the Iberian Peninsula. This is a beautiful way for you and your loved one to take in the sights of Lisbon from the water, including the Belém Tower and the Cristo Rei Statue.

Where to Eat in Lisbon

Palácio Chiado

Address: Rua do Alecrim 70, 1200-018 Lisbon
Hours of operation

- Monday to Wednesday: 12:30 p.m. to 12 a.m.
- Thursday to Sunday: 12 p.m. to 2 a.m.

If you want a romantic evening out, Palácio Chiado will give you just that. This restaurant offers a unique dining experience in a restored 18th-century palace. At this restaurant, you can enjoy a diverse menu featuring traditional Portuguese cuisine and other European flavors served in the various dining spaces around the building. In addition to a fantastic gastronomy experience, Palácio Chiado is open late on the weekends so that you can enjoy a wide range of drinks and cocktails at the bars around the establishment.

Seen

Address: Hotel Tivoli Av. da Liberdade 185, 1250-147 Lisbon (on the ninth floor)
Hours of operation

- Sunday to Thursday: 6:30 p.m. to 1 a.m.
- Friday and Saturday: 6:30 p.m. to 2 a.m.

Seen is a stylish rooftop restaurant on the ninth floor of the Hotel Tivoli Avenida Liberdade. It offers an unforgettable dining experience alongside stunning city views. The restaurant provides Portuguese, Japanese, and Brazilian-inspired dishes in a sleek ambiance that combines lush greenery with an Art Deco style. In addition to the fantastic dishes cooked by Chef Olivier da Costa, you can enjoy innovative cocktails with your meal. It is a romantic and social restaurant you don't want to miss!

Bairro do Avillez

Address: Rua Nova da Trindade 18, Lisbon 1200-303
Hours of operation

- The tavern and terrace is open daily from 12 p.m. to 12 a.m.
- The patio is open daily from 12 a.m. to 3 p.m. and 6:30 p.m. to 11 p.m.
- The mini bar is open Sunday through Wednesday from 7 p.m. to 1 a.m., Thursday from 7 p.m. to 2 a.m., and Fridays and Saturdays from 7 p.m. to 3:30 a.m.
- The Pizzeria is open Monday to Friday from 6:30 p.m. to 11 p.m. and Saturday and Sunday from 12:30 p.m. to 3 p.m. and 6:30 p.m. to 11 p.m.

Bairro do Avillez, founded by Chef José Avillez, features affordable and mid-range options to cater to anyone's budget. This restaurant offers various dishes, from traditional Portuguese cuisine to pizza. It is also a great bar to go to if you're looking for a late-night drink.

A Cultura do Hamburguer

Address: Rua Salgadeiras 38, Lisbon 1200-396
Hours of operation: 12 p.m. to 12 a.m. daily

A Cultura do Hamburguer is a popular establishment for those who love burgers at a great price. This casual eatery offers various burger options, focusing on engaging, flavorful combinations. The prices are cheap, which is great for eating lunch without breaking the bank!

Lisboa à Noite

Address: Rua das Gaveas 69 Bairro Alto, Lisbon 1200-206
Hours of operation: 7:30 p.m. to 12 a.m. daily

Lisboa à Noite is another beautiful and romantic restaurant option for the romantics reading this book! This establishment is in a former horse stable with tiled panels dating back to the 1700s. At this restaurant, you can feast upon classic Portuguese dishes, including seafood, stews, and grilled fish.

What to Eat in Lisbon

Pastéis de Nata

These iconic custard tarts are a staple of Lisbon's culinary scene. Encased in a flaky pastry shell, the creamy custard filling melts in your mouth, delicately sweetened and dusted with a hint of cinnamon. Whether enjoyed fresh from the oven or paired with a cup of coffee, Pastéis de Nata offers a delightful taste of Portugal's rich pastry tradition.

Bacalhau à Brás

A beloved Portuguese dish, Bacalhau à Brás features tender flakes of salted cod combined with sautéed onions, thinly sliced potatoes, and scrambled eggs. The ingredients are expertly seasoned with garlic and parsley, resulting in a harmonious blend of flavors that is both comforting and satisfying.

Francesinha

This hearty sandwich is a culinary indulgence not to be missed in Lisbon. Layers of ham, linguica sausage, and thinly sliced steak are sandwiched between slices of bread, then smothered in melted cheese and topped with a fried egg. The entire creation is bathed in a spicy tomato and beer-based sauce, creating a symphony of flavors that will leave you craving more.

Arroz de Marisco

A quintessential Portuguese seafood dish, Arroz de Marisco features a flavorful rice stew brimming with an assortment of fresh seafood. Clams, shrimp, and mussels are simmered in a fragrant broth infused with tomatoes, garlic, and aromatic spices. The result is a comforting and satisfying dish that perfectly captures the essence of Lisbon's coastal cuisine.

Sardinhas Assadas

Grilled sardines are a beloved delicacy in Lisbon, showcasing the city's deep connection to the sea. Fresh sardines are seasoned simply with salt, pepper, and olive oil before being grilled to perfection. The tender, flavorful fish is typically served with a side of roasted potatoes or crusty bread, offering a taste of Portugal's maritime heritage in every bite.

Where to Stay in Lisbon

Memmo Alfama

Address: Travessa das Merceeiras, 27 – Alfama, Lisbon 1100-348

Memmo Alfama is a romantic accommodation option set in a 19th-century building in the Alfama District. The rooms feature a minimalist look with neutral tones to enhance the relaxed ambiance.

In addition to comfortable rooms, Memmo Alfama has a wine bar with beautiful views of the Tagus River. This wine bar also serves light meals to enjoy alongside your wine. There is also an outdoor pool at this establishment.

If you stay here, you will be near several of Lisbon's attractions, including São Jorge Castle and Commerce Square.

Pensão Amor Madam's Lodge

Address: 38 Rua Nova do Carvalho, Misericordia, Lisbon 1200-292

Pensão Amor Madam's Lodge is situated in the vibrant Cais do Sodré neighborhood and has some of the coolest rooms decked out in deep reds and vintage-inspired decor, creating a romantic ambiance. Beyond the rooms, this hotel is within walking distance of many attractions, including Commerce Square and Museu do Fado.

Lisbon Story Guesthouse

Address: Largo De São Domingos, 18 S/L, Arroios, Lisbon 1150-320

Lisbon Story Guesthouse is a budget-friendly option in Lisbon, offering a self-catering option with the ability to use the shared kitchen. The rooms feature private or shared bathrooms. Staying here will put you near attractions such as Museu do Fado.

LX51 Studios & Suites by APT IIN

Address: Avenida Duque de Loule, 51, Santo Antonio, Lisbon 1050-087

LX51 Studios & Suites by APT IIN is in the San Antonio District, offering well-equipped studios and suites designed for long and short stays. The rooms are decorated in a contemporary style, and if you stay in a studio, you'll have a small kitchenette with a fridge and a microwave. Staying here will put you within walking distance of several popular attractions in Lisbon, including Commerce Square and Eduardo VII Park.

Masa Hotel 5 de Outubro

Address: Avenida 5 de Outubro N°87, Avenidas Novas, Lisbon 1050-050

Masa Hotel 5 de Outubro is a three-star hotel in Lisbon's heart. This hotel boasts modern rooms with a comfortable space to relax after a day of exploring the city. If you stay here, you will be within several attractions, including Eduardo VII Park, the historic and bustling Marquês de Pombal Square, Jardim do Campo Grande, and Calouste Gulbenkian Museum.

What Not to Do in Lisbon

Don't Expect the Lisbon Cathedral to be Grand

While most churches in Portugal are beautiful and boast a rich history, the Lisbon Cathedral is surprisingly not as exquisite as some churches you may visit while on your trip. It's worth admiring from the outside, but you won't be overly wowed if you go inside. So, maybe save the admission fee for a different church or other attraction that interests you.

Don't Ride the Santa Justa Lift

The Santa Justa Lift is simply an elevator that will take you from Baixa to the viewpoint over Carmo Square. While it has a style similar to the Eiffel Tower, as the Portuguese engineer who designed it also worked alongside Gustave Eiffel, it's nothing spectacular. Plus, it is €5.50 to ride, and you'll spend more time in line waiting to ride it up. That said, the viewpoint is worth going to, but you can use an elevator on Rua do Carmo, which costs around €1.50 and is not crammed with people.

Don't Eat on Famous Streets

Many top tourist areas like Portas de Santo Antão Street will have restaurants. You're better off avoiding places overrun with tourists, as menu prices will be much higher. Of course, the rule of thumb is always to look up the places you want to go and check out the reviews of other patrons who have eaten at the establishments to know if it is worth the money or time.

Don't Try 'Pastéis De Nata' At The Wrong Places

Don't assume that you will get similar quality 'pastéis de nata' desserts everywhere, and try to have them in the first store you find. Portuguese treat the pastéis de nata as a national patrimony, and there are must-go places for the perfect dessert. The best options in Lisbon are Pastéis de Belém and stores like Manteigaria or Aloma.

Don't Forget To Say 'Obrigado'

Many travelers are not aware that in Portuguese, the way you say 'thank you' is based on the speaker and not on the one spoken to. Women say 'obrigada,' and men say 'obrigado.' Most travelers mess with this etiquette due to a lack of knowledge. By the way, do NOT say 'gracias' even by mistake.

Don't Rent a Car in Lisbon

Do not rent a car in Lisbon. Its recommended to explore the city center on foot. It's a city which you can explore better on foot in order to discover the old neighborhoods like Mouraria, Alfama, Graça, Madragoa, etc. This is not possible to do by car, and it will make it difficult for you to discover true gems that are only reachable on foot.

Keep in Mind certain Food Etiquette.

Traveller needs to keep in mind certain food etiquette. Never eat sardines with a fork and knife. Sardines are savored with hands. Also don't eat pastéis de bacalhau with cooking cream.

Next Stop: Porto

Lisbon is one of the first cities many might think of when they think of Portugal, and that's likely because of its rich history and culture dating back centuries and its stunning architecture spanning back to the Moorish times. In this chapter, we have explored many of the areas worth visiting, including some ideas to make your trip more romantic if you travel to Portugal with your significant other. If Lisbon will be one of your stops on your Portuguese trip, start thinking about your itinerary and the top places you want to visit in this iconic city.

Now that we have unveiled Lisbon's secrets, it is time to head north to Porto, where the wine seems to flow as freely as the gorgeous Duro River. Porto has charming characteristics, historical pieces to explore, and some things to avoid. Let's continue our journey around Portugal, where more adventure will be had.

Chapter 4:

Porto —Dos and Don'ts

P Orto is a beautiful city steeped in history within the nooks and crannies of the streets and alleyways. Porto has a rich culture where its age-old traditions intertwine with modern innovation. Whether wandering through the winding streets adorned with colorful tiles or enjoying the rich flavors of local cuisine, this old city has an enchanting atmosphere. Let's explore the different ways you can immerse yourself in what Porto offers while steering clear of some things that won't add value to your time in this iconic Portuguese city.

Discovering Porto

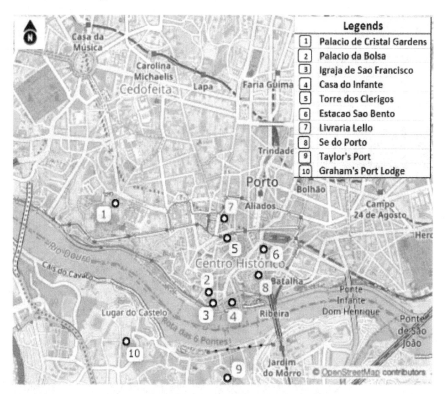

Porto is Portugal's second-largest city, with beautiful neighborhoods, villas along the Douro River, and quaint cobbled streets. In 1996, it was named a UNESCO

World Heritage Site due to its history and significant landmarks, including the Dom Luís I Bridge, which spans the river and offers fantastic panoramic views of Porto.

While visiting Poro, you can take in the sights of Palácio de Cristal Gardens, Palácio da Bolsa, and the intricate tiles at São Bento Station and around the city. Porto is also renowned for its port wine production, with many cellars where you can taste the fortified wine. Whether wandering through Porto's historic quarters, enjoying delicious Portuguese cuisine, or taking a romantic sunset cruise with your significant other, the city's unforgettable charm will enchant you as you travel around its beautiful streets.

What to Do in Porto

Palácio de Cristal Gardens

Address: Rúa Don Manuel II, Porto 4250-260

Hours of operation

- October to March: 8 a.m. to 7 p.m.
- April to September: 8 a.m. to 9 p.m.

The Palácio de Cristal Gardens (Crystal Palace Gardens) are a wonderful place to escape the hustle and bustle of Porto's city life. Designed by Émile Davis in the 19th century, these expansive gardens are well-loved for their beautiful green spaces, fountains, ponds, vibrant floral displays, and stunning river and Atlantic Ocean views. Take a stroll or sit on one of the many benches as you take in the historical sights of this beautiful garden. If you're visiting Portugal with your significant other, a picnic is also a great way to visit Palácio de Cristal Gardens, a romantic one.

Palácio da Bolsa

Address: Rúa de Ferreira Borges, Porto 4050-253

Hours of operation
- April to October: 9 a.m. to 6:30 p.m.
- November to March: 9 a.m. to 12:30 p.m.

The Palácio da Bolsa (Stock Exchange Palace) is one of the most beautiful buildings in Porto. Built-in the 19th century on the former Saint Francis Convent ruins, the Palácio da Bolsa was initially intended as a new stock exchange to support Porto's growing economy and financial needs. However, it took 50 years to complete due to several setbacks, so it wasn't inaugurated until 1891.

The Neoclassical building features attractive façades, intricate carvings, and more. The highlights of this palace are the Arab Room, a stunning chamber featuring Moorish-inspired motifs; the Golden Room, where you can view elaborate decorations and historical artifacts; and the Assembly Room, which looks like it is fully decorated with wood.

You can only visit the Palácio da Bolsa by joining a guided tour. Guided tours are 90 minutes long.

Ticket type	Price
Adults	€ 12
Students and seniors	€ 7.50
Children 12 years old and under	Free

Igreja de São Francisco

Address: Rua do Infante Dom Henrique, Porto 4050-297

Hours of operation
- Summer: 9 a.m. to 6:30 p.m.
- Winter: 9 a.m. to 5 p.m.

The Igreja de São Francisco (Church of São Francisco) is one of Porto's most culturally rich cathedrals. The construction of this church began in 1245 and underwent several renovations over the centuries, resulting in a stunning blend of architectural styles, including Gothic and Baroque. Inside the church, you'll be able to see and admire the intricate wood carvings, altarpieces, and ornate tilework. The highlight of the interior is the Tree of Jesse, hand-carved by Filipe Silva and Antonio Gomes to reflect Jesus's family tree. The catacombs are also an exciting place to visit under the church. There, you'll see the final resting places of the Franciscan monks and the members of wealthy Porto families. There is also an ossuary covered with human bones and skulls, which you can see through the glass floor. It seems morbid but serves as a reminder of the circle of life.

Ticket type	Price
Adult	€ 6
Students up to 25 years old and seniors 65 and up	€ 4
Family (two adults and students)	€ 15
Children 12 years old and under	Free

Fundação de Serralves

Address: Rua Dom João de Castro 210, Porto 4150-417

Hours of operation: 10 a.m. to 7 p.m. daily

The history of Serralves dates back to the vision of Carlos Alberto Cabral, the second Count of Vizela. During the 20th century, the Count acquired the large estate of the Fundação de Serralves (Serralves Foundation). He intended to transform the property into a place showcasing the best Portuguese art, culture, and landscape design, which you will see today. The centerpiece is the Serralves House, a great example of Art Deco architecture. It was once where artwork from Portuguese and international artists was on display until the museum opened in 1996. This is a great cultural experience in Porto, especially if you are a fan of art. Tickets to the Fundação de Serralves are €24 per adult and free for children 12 and under.

Casa do Infante

Address: Rua da Alfândega 10, Porto 4050-029

Hours of operation: 9:30 a.m. to 1 p.m. and 2 p.m. to 5:30 p.m. (closed on Mondays)

Casa do Infante (Infante's House) is a significant historical landmark in Porto dating back to 1325. It was given its name in 1394 when Henry the Navigator (Prince Henry) was born. He was a significant figure during the Age of Discovery. The building served as a royal residence for Portuguese royal families to stay when visiting Porto. However, since then, it has become a museum where you can view the exciting architecture inside, and it has undergone several renovations. This attraction is €2.20 per person, but if you go on Saturdays or Sundays, it's free.

Torre dos Clérigos

Address: Rua de São Filipe de Nery, Porto 4050-546

Hours of operation: 9 a.m. to 7 p.m. daily except for the following dates:

- December 24: 9 a.m. to 2 p.m.
- December 25: 11 a.m. to 7 p.m.
- December 31: 9 a.m. to 2 p.m.
- January 1: 11 a.m. to 7 p.m.
- The last entrance is 30 minutes before closing.
- Night pass for the tower: 7 p.m. to 11 p.m.

The Torre dos Clérigos (Clérigos Tower), Porto's most iconic symbol, towers 249 feet above the city. The tower was designed by Italian architect Nicolau Nasoni and was built between 1754 and 1763 with funding provided by the Brotherhood of the

Clérgios (hence its name). The tower and the church are beautiful reflections of Baroque architecture, with motifs to discover while visiting. If you choose to climb the building, it is 240 steps to the top, and you will be rewarded with fantastic views of Porto's city center and the Douro River. Your ticket will also give you access to the Museum of the Brotherhood of the Clerics, where you can see collections of religious artwork, furniture, and sculptures between the 13th and 20th centuries.

Ticket type	Price
Adult - Tower and Clérgios Museum	€ 8
Student -Tower and Clérgios Museum	€ 5
Guided tour of the Clérgios Museum, church, and tower	€ 9.50
Night pass	€ 5
Children 10 years old and under	Free

Estação São Bento

Address: Praça de Almeida Garrett, Porto 4000-069

Estação São Bento (São Bento Station) is Porto's historic railway station in Portugal's heart. The station dates back to the 20th century when the first train arrived in 1896; however, it wasn't officially established until 1916. Nonetheless, the station is renowned for its stunning neoclassical façade and more than 20,000 tiles decorating the hall, all hand-illustrated to show the critical historical moments in Portugal's history. This station is arguably one of the most beautiful train stations in the world and will be your central transportation hub if you arrive at or leave Porto by train.

Livraria Lello

Address: Rua das Carmelitas 144, neoclassical 4050-161

Hours of operation: 9 a.m. to 7:30 p.m. daily (closed on holidays)

Livraria Lello (Lello Bookstore) is a haven for book lovers who appreciate beautiful bookstores. Founded in 1906, it is renowned for its neo-Gothic architecture and ornate interior design. The exterior of the bookstore features intricate carvings and stained-glass windows that let in sunlight. You'll find a stunning red staircase leading to the second floor. Some even think this bookstore inspired Hogwarts School of Witchcraft and Wizardry in J.K. Rowling's Harry Potter series.

If you intend to visit Livraria Lello, the fee is €8, which can be redeemed as a book discount. The fee helps manage the bookstore's high tourism demand and preserve the establishment.

Sé do Porto

Address: Terreiro da Sé, Porto 4050-573

Hours of operation
- April to October: 9 a.m. to 6:30 p.m.
- November to March: 9 a.m. to 5:30 p.m.
- Closed on Christmas and Easter

Sé do Porto, also known as Porto Cathedral, is one of the significant cathedrals in Porto, dating back to the 12th century. This cathedral showcases several architectural styles and has been renovated several times throughout the centuries. Thus, you'll see architectural nods to the Romanesque, Gothic, and Baroque periods. While exploring the cathedral, entering the cloister next to the temple is worth it. This area was built sometime in the 14th century and is adorned with painted tiles reflecting scenes from the bible. It's a small fee but worth it when you can take in more tile artwork!

Ticket type	Price
Cathedral	Free
Cloister	€ 3
Children up to 10 years old	Free

Port Cellar Wine Tours

Porto is famous for its port wine, so visiting some port wine cellars while visiting the city is worth visiting. You must be at least 18 years old to enjoy wine at any of the cellars.

Sandeman's Wine Cellar

Address: Largo Miguel Bombarda, 4430-175 Vila Nova de Gaia

Hours of operation

- Monday to Saturday: 10 a.m. to 12:30 p.m. and 2 p.m. to 6 p.m.
- Sunday: 10 a.m. to 12:30 p.m. and 2 p.m. to 7:30 p.m.

Sandeman's Wine Cellar is one of the oldest wine cellars to visit while in Porto. Located in Vila Nova de Gaia, this wine cellar was opened in 1790 by Sandeman, and tours will bring you through the establishment's history and how they produce their port wine. Here are all of the tours available:

Sandeman 1790 Visit: During the Sandeman 1790 Visit, you will be taken on a historical journey back to when the wine cellar was established. You will learn about Sandeman's roots and how they were advertised during earlier eras. This tour will finish in the 1790 Room, where you can taste five port wines.

Sandeman Old Tawnies Visit: The Sandeman Old Tawnies Visit will bring you through the history of Sandeman and the traditions that go into creating their port wines. This tour will end with a tasting of four award-winning port wines.

Porto Sandeman Visit: During the Porto Sandeman Visit, you'll be brought through rows of casks and vats where the port wine is aged and finished, and you'll taste three styles of port from the last 40 years.

Mastering Sandeman Port Wine: This is an experience you can take at the wine cellar. You will dive deeper into what makes this type of wine unique, how it is produced, the Douro Region, and how to taste the five selected port wines like a master.

Porto Sandeman Exclusive Experience: During the Porto Sandeman Exclusive Experience, you will learn about Sandeman's chronological history and production processes and taste six port wines.

Tour type	Length of time	Price
Sandeman 1790 Visit	90 min	€ 28
Sandeman Old Tawnies Visit	90 min	€ 48
Porto Sandeman Visit	90 min	€ 21
Mastering Sandeman Port Wine	90 min	€ 68
Porto Sandeman Exclusive Experience	2.5 hrs	€ 160

Taylor's Port

Address: Rua do Choupelo 250, 4400-088 Vila Nova de Gaia

Hours of operation

- Cellars: 10 a.m. to 6:15 p.m. daily
- Tasting room and shop: 10 a.m. to 7:30 p.m. daily
- Restaurant: 12:30 p.m. to 3 p.m. and 7 p.m. to 10 p.m.

Taylor's Port, also known as Taylor's Fladgate, is the oldest port winemaker in the Porto region. You are invited to explore this establishment's historic lodges and cellars, where they have produced port wine for over 300 years. Tours of Taylor's Port are self-guided, with audio in 13 languages. You will enjoy two port wines at the end of your self-guided tour.

Ticket type	Price
Adults (18 years old and up)	€ 20
Children (8 to 17 years old)	€ 7.50
Children under 8	Free
Family (two adults and two children between 8 and 17 years old)	€ 50

Graham's Port Lodge

Address: Rua de Agro 141, 4400-351 Vila Nova de Gaia

Hours of operation

- April 1 to October 31: 10 a.m. to 5:30 p.m.
- November 1 to March 31: 10 a.m. to 5 p.m. (tastings are available until 5:30 p.m.)

Graham's Port Lodge invites you to enjoy an enriching wine tour experience at their establishment, which has been around since 1820. You will be taken behind the scenes at Graham's Port Lodge, where you will hear about the methods and techniques used in making their version of this iconic wine. After the tour, you can taste some of their ports while enjoying panoramic views of Porto from the lodge's terrace. All tours must be booked in advance, starting at €50 per person and going up to €250 per person.

If you want to enhance your port-tasting experience, Graham's Port offers a world-class gastronomic experience. This experience includes a lodge tour and tasting their port wine. It ends with lunch at Vinum Restaurant. The cost is €115 per person.

Neighborhoods to Explore in Porto

Ribeira

Ribeira is one of Porto's oldest neighborhoods to explore, with plenty of historical significance among its brightly colored buildings, many adorned with flowers and other plants on the balconies. In addition to the beautiful buildings, Ribeira served as a large commercial center dating back to the Roman era. In your exploration, you may see many old warehouse buildings, though many have fallen into disrepair.

As you wander through the narrow, cobbled streets, you will have many opportunities to stop and take in the picturesque views of the riverfront and watch as the anchored boats bob in the river. Numerous cafés, restaurants, and bars dot the area and along the riverfront, and many have outdoor seating, which will make for a lovely stop to enjoy a drink or a small bite to eat and simply be with the atmosphere.

Sé

Like Ribeira, Sé is another ancient neighborhood in Porto, boasting plenty of architecture to admire. The starting point for exploring Sé is Sé do Porto, where you will wander through the maze-like streets with colorful houses and lovely cafés. This neighborhood also includes the Palácio da Bolsa.

Baixa

Baixa is Porto's bustling neighborhood, surrounded by beautiful streets with shops, cafés, and restaurants. This is where you'll find famous landmarks like the São Bento Station and the Praça da Liberdade square, where many will gather for special events. The square is also a great central point that leads you to other points of interest in Porto. Additionally. You can explore the bustling Mercado do Balhão market, where you can pick up fresh produce, meats, and other local delicacies. For art, music, or fashion lovers, you will want to explore the Quarteirão das Artes, where you'll find several galleries and boutique shops selling the latest European trends.

Cedofeita and Miragaia

Cedofeita and Miragaia are two neighborhoods adjacent to one another, offering you a chance to experience Porto as a local. Cedofeita is known for its bohemian atmosphere, where you can shop at trendy boutiques, see some eclectic street art, and enjoy lunch or a beverage at one of their lovely small cafés. If you wander along the Rua Miguel Bombarda, you will find a collection of art galleries you can peruse. On Saturdays, a Porto Belo Market is a great time to pick up unique souvenirs.

In contrast, Miragaia is steeped in history, with narrow alleys and picturesque squares that will take you back in time. This neighborhood was once a medieval Jewish corner, and as you follow the staircases, you'll eventually find a wall dating back to the 14th century that once protected Porto.

Both areas have unique charms, especially since they are next to each other. If you come to one of the overlooks in the evening, bring your drink to enjoy as you watch the sunset with the locals.

Vila Nova de Gaia

Technically speaking, Vila Nova de Gaia isn't part of Porto—it's its own city. Located on the other side of the Dom Luís I Bridge, Vila Nova de Gaia offers great views of Ribeira along the riverside promenade. This is also the neighborhood to visit if you want to explore several iconic wine lodges, including some discussed earlier in this chapter (Graham's Port Lodge, Taylor's Port, and Sandeman Port

Cellar). There are also several cafés, restaurants, and shops you can pop into to try the local cuisine or purchase artisanal goods.

Romantic Spots in Porto

Picnic in Serralves Park

Serralves Park is part of the Serralves Contemporary Museum and is a beautiful area to enjoy a picnic with your significant other, especially since different trees bloom throughout the year. If you plan to visit Fundação de Serralves, this is worth it.

Sunset at Serra do Pilar

If you happen to be exploring Vila Nova de Gaia, it is worth going to the Serra do Pilar. This landmark gives you an incredible view of the river and Porto and a chance to watch the sunset. It's a popular spot, so try to get there early!

Romantic Dinner at a Port Wine Cellar

It's easy to plan a romantic dinner, but what if you take the romance up a notch and have a fado concert *while* you and your partner are dining? For those who are looking to propose, this idea is for you! You can book a romantic dinner with an intimate fado concert at Fonseca Cellars. This cellar will create a beautiful dinner paired with port and other wine as you enjoy the live music in an intimate setting. This cellar is over 200 years old and one you should consider looking into for a romantic dinner.

Where to Stay in Porto

Exmo Hotel by Olivia

Address: Rua do Infante Dom Henrique 55-61, União de Freguesias do Centro, Porto 4050-297

Exmo Hotel by Olivia is a quaint boutique near the riverfront in Porto. This four-star hotel features a rustic look with stone walls and Scandinavian-style decor with city and river views. Some rooms also come with a balcony overlooking the river. This hotel will be within walking distance of attractions, including Ribeira Square, Palácio da Bolsa (Stock Exchange Palace), and Torre dos Clérigos (Clérigos Tower). This hotel also has a buffet breakfast to make starting your day easy. You're also welcome to enjoy a cocktail or a glass of wine at their on-site bar in the evenings.

Mouzinho 160

Address: Rua Mouzinho da Silveira 160, União de Freguesias do Centro, Porto 4050-416

If you are a traveler who prefers a self-catering option, Mouzinho 160 is an excellent choice for accommodations in Porto. This accommodation is in a renovated 19th-century building with spacious apartments and a small kitchenette where you can cook some of your meals to save money. A few apartment options are available; some have a terrace or a balcony. If you stay here, you will be close to several attractions, including Praça dos Clérigos (Clérigos Square) and Palácio de Cristal Gardens (Crystal Palace Gardens).

The Lodge Hotel

Address: Rua Serpa Pinto 60, Vila Nova de Gaia 4400-307

If you're looking for a luxury stay for you and your significant other to indulge in fancy accommodation, check out The Lodge Hotel. Situated atop a hill, The Lodge Hotel offers excellent views of Porto. It is a short walk or drive to various attractions, including Palácio de Cristal Gardens (Crystal Palace Gardens), Ponte Maria Pia (Maria Pia Bridge), and Torre dos Clérigos (Clerigos Tower). This hotel offers a wide range of amenities to enhance your stay, including a fitness center, pool, and a restaurant serving delicious Portuguese dishes.

The House Of Sandeman

Address: Largo Miguel Bombarda, Vila Nova de Gaia 4430-175

The House Of Sandeman is the world's first hostel in the historic Port Wine Cellars of Sandeman building. This hostel is mid-range; you can stay in a dormitory or double room. No matter which option you choose, you will have scenic views of Porto and the Douro River. Additionally, there is a restaurant on site where you can listen to live music on some nights. Many of Porto's attractions are a short walk or drive from the hostel, including São Bento Train Station and Casa do Infante.

Porto Alegria Garden

Address: Rua da Alegria 508, Bonfim, Porto 4000-035

Porto Alegria Garden is an affordable accommodation in the historic Bonfim district in a renovated 19th-century building. Inside this beautiful hotel, you'll find it adorned with classic decorations and furnished with antique furniture. Each room has a seating area and a small kitchenette; some rooms have a terrace leading to the garden. You are also welcome to have breakfast delivered to your room to eat on your patio if you'd like, or you can enjoy it in the garden.

Where to Eat in Porto

A Margarida Leça da Palmeira

Address: Rua do Castelo 59, Leça da Palmeira 4450-632

Hours of operation
- Tuesday to Thursday: 12:30 p.m. to 3 p.m. and 7:30 p.m. to 11 p.m.
- Friday and Saturday: 12:30 p.m. to 3:30 p.m. and 7:30 p.m. to 12 a.m.

A Margarida Leça da Palmeira is a family-owned restaurant with over two decades of service offering patrons authentic Portuguese cuisine. This restaurant is along the Leça da Palmeira, offering great views of the North Atlantic Ocean while you feast on seafood, fish, steak, and more. Prices are a little more expensive, but it will make for a lovely night out if you're seeking somewhere with a casual vibe.

O Buraco

Address: Rua Bolhao 95, Porto 4000-112

Hours of operation: 12 p.m. to 3 p.m. and 7 p.m. to 10 p.m. (It is only open for lunch on Saturdays and is closed on Sundays.)

O Buraco is a cozy and popular budget-friendly restaurant serving homemade hearty Portuguese dishes at lunch and dinner. You may need to wait, especially if you'd like to stop here to eat lunch, but it's worth it for their menu. Some popular options include veal pie, duck rice, and *tripas* (tripe stew).

Taberna Santo António

Address: Rua Virtudes 32, Porto 4050-630

Hours of operation
- Tuesday to Saturday: 11 a.m. to 10 p.m.
- Sunday: 11 a.m. to 4 p.m.

Taberna Santo António is a cozy restaurant renowned for its simple and flavorful Portuguese dishes. It is situated in the pretty neighborhood of Miragaia and offers a relaxed atmosphere in which to enjoy your meal. The daily specials are highly recommended, as they never disappoint. If you have a sweet tooth, their chocolate mousse is one of the best in Porto. The prices are low here, too, so you won't have to worry about breaking your budget!

O Ernesto

Address: Rua da Picaria 85, Porto 4050-478

Hours of operation
- Monday: 12 p.m. to 3 p.m.
- Tuesday to Saturday: 12 p.m. to 3 p.m. and 7:15 p.m. to 10 p.m.

O Ernesto is another cozy restaurant known for its simple Portuguese cuisine. Here, you will find a variety of traditional Portuguese dishes, with a big focus on grilled seafood and locally sourced meats. This restaurant is about mid-range and has a great selection of wine to pair with your meal.

A Cozinha do Manel

Address: Rua do Heroismo 215, Porto 4300-259

Hours of operation
- Tuesday to Saturday: 12:30 p.m. to 3 p.m. and 7:30 p.m. to 10 p.m.
- Sunday: 12:30 p.m. to 3 p.m.

A Cozinha do Manel is a casual eatery with traditional Portuguese decor. This restaurant has been open for over 30 years and has seen many famous faces come through its doors to enjoy the dishes at this establishment. The servings are small (like tapas), and everything is perfectly cooked, making A Cozinha do Manel a great place to eat if you want to share a few things.

What to Eat in Porto

Bacalhau à Gomes de Sá

This classic Portuguese dish showcases salted cod, known as bacalhau, sautéed with onions, garlic, and potatoes, then baked to golden perfection. The result is a comforting and flavorful dish that pays homage to Porto's maritime heritage.

Tripas à Moda do Porto

Known as "Porto-style tripe," this traditional dish is a testament to the city's culinary history. It features tripe, beans, and various meats, such as chorizo and pork, slow-cooked with aromatic spices until tender and flavorful. Served with rice, this hearty dish is a beloved comfort food in Porto.

Caldo Verde

This simple yet comforting soup is a staple of Portuguese cuisine, featuring thinly sliced kale, potatoes, and chorizo simmered in a flavorful broth. Served piping hot with a drizzle of olive oil, Caldo Verde is the perfect way to warm up on a chilly evening in Porto.

Arroz de Tamboril

This aromatic rice dish features monkfish cooked with tomatoes, onions, garlic, and rice, infused with the flavors of saffron and fresh herbs. Served with a squeeze of lemon, Arroz de Tamboril is a seafood lover's delight, showcasing Porto's fresh coastal ingredients.

What Not to Do in Porto

Try to Avoid Visiting Porto In Summer

If you want to avoid the crowded areas in Porto, plan to visit when less busy. Like other places in Europe, Porto tends to get very crowded during the summer months. While summer is a great time to visit the beaches of Porto and enjoy festivals, you'll have to manage the big crowds. Instead, it's recommended to visit during the spring or autumn. The weather is still warm, and fewer travelers visit Porto during this period, so you'll get a much better relaxed experience.

Avoid Staying in the City Center

One of the best ways to avoid crowds in Porto is to explore areas further out of the city center. Ribeira is at the heart of the Old Town, and while it's a wonderful place to visit, the busy crowds make it less enjoyable during the day. If you're not a fan of nightlife, you'll also want to skip Baix. It can get quite busy in the evening.

Instead of the city center, it's recommended to search for accommodation in the relatively quiet neighborhood of Miragaia, which is set alongside the river. This neighborhood was outside the city walls around the 15th century and was home to large Armenian and Jewish communities. If you want to be closer to the important landmarks, Bonfim makes a good base. It's a mostly residential area with easy links to the city center. Instead of typical tourist attractions, you'll find cozy eateries and shops to explore.

Don't Just Stop at the Tiles in São Beno Train Station

As you know, São Bento Train has some remarkable *azulejos* tiles that make a beautiful masterpiece inside the station. However, this isn't the only place that has tiles. You'll see them in many places around the city, including along the historic Santa Catarina.

Don't Go Shopping in Rua Santa Catarina

If you head along Santa Catarina, you can look for tiled buildings, but it is not a great place to shop. Many stores along this road, such as Zara, are found worldwide. If you want to shop for something authentic in Portugal or Porto, check out Cedofeita instead.

Don't Use the Guindais Elevator in Both Directions

If you want to explore the Batalha and Ribeira neighborhoods, one of the best and most efficient ways to get to one from the other is to use the Guindais Elevator. It is a pretty ride, especially if you're trying to get to the upper side of Porto fast. However, when you're done, use the Guindas or Codeçal staircases to get back down. They are antique steps and a way to immerse yourself in the daily life of Porto.

Don't Drive in Porto

Porto is small enough that you can get around the city on foot. You'll also get your steps in and see more of the city than you would if you were in a car. Additionally, it saves you the big headache of trying to find parking or worrying about driving if you sample port wine.

Buy an Andante Card and Use public transportation.

Porto has a good public transportation system, with six metro lines linking districts across town. You can also take the metro to the beach and the airport (Violet Line E). In addition to the metro, there are buses, trams, and even one funicular. For convenience, purchase an Andante Card and use it on the metro and buses.

Be Mindful of Pickpocketers

Porto is a safe city, and the crime rate is low. But pickpocketing and bag snatching are the main concerns to be aware of, especially when traveling on the trams and metro. Try to avoid traveling during crowded peak times. At night, avoid walking around the dark alleys of the Ribeira and near the São Bento train station. You should take a taxi at nighttime.

Next Stop: Cascais, Coimbra, and Braga

In this chapter, we explored the beautiful city of Porto, situated alongside the historic Douro River. This iconic city has many things to see and do, whether you're exploring Europe alone or traveling with your partner. Get a glimpse at what makes Porto so unique. With these ideas in mind, you now know what to add to your itinerary if you plan to visit Porto while in Portugal.

In the next chapter, we will explore Cascais, Coimbra, and Braga, where you can explore these charming towns, each with its unique history and enchanting atmosphere.

Chapter 5:

Cascais, Coimbra and Braga —Dos and Don'ts

P ortugal has many hidden gems along its coastlines and in the heart of the country. In this chapter, we'll explore three iconic and diverse towns: Cascais, Coimbra, and Braga, each with its own historical narrative, charm, and romance.

Discovering Cascais, Coimbra, and Braga

Cascais, Coimbra, and Braga each offer a distinct slice of Portuguese culture, history, and beauty. Situated along the coastline of Portugal (and not too far from Lisbon), Cascais is renowned for its beautiful beaches, charming old town, and vibrant cultural scene. This Portuguese town is a popular choice in the summer for those wanting to soak up the sunshine, surf, and enjoy drinks on the patios of numerous cafés. Beyond the beaches, Cascais is home to some impressive landmarks to explore, including Museu Condes de Castro Guimarães (Condes de Castro Guimarães Museum), Boca do Inferno (Hell's Mouth), and Farol e Museu de Santa Marta (Santa Marta Lighthouse and Museum) showcasing Cascais's stunning landscape and importance in maritime history. While in this Portuguese town, it is also great to wander through the winding streets of the old town, where you can admire the colorful buildings and shop in various boutiques.

In the heart of Portugal is where you will find the historic city of Coimbra, home to one of the oldest universities in Europe. Coimbra University is a UNESCO World Heritage Site and dominates Coimbra's city skyline with its impressive Baroque architecture. This university is worth exploring, especially for those who love literature, with the library containing an expansive collection of books, some of which are rare. At one point, Coimbra served as the medieval capital of Portugal for more than 100 years, allowing you to glimpse into its former life, especially if you follow the medieval streets along Alta.

In the northern region lies Braga, a city known for its religious tradition and fantastic architecture. Also known as the "Rome of Portugal," Braga is where the first church was constructed in the country, and the Santuario do Bom Jesus do Monte, where you can take in incredible city views. Beyond the religious history and landmarks, Braga is a great place to immerse yourself in the daily lives of the locals by going to various markets or enjoying a drink or small snack at one of the cafés.

Whichever of the three towns you visit, you'll get a different glimpse into Portugal's history and culture, giving you a different adventure than visiting the major Portuguese cities.

What to Do in Cascais

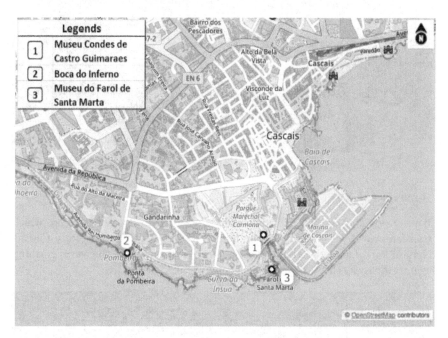

Museu Condes de Castro Guimarães

Address: Avenida Rei Humberto II de Itália, Parque Marechal Carmona, Cascais 2750–319

Hours of operation

- Tuesday to Friday: 10 a.m. to 6 p.m.
- Saturdays, Sundays, and holidays: 10 a.m. to 1 p.m. and 2 p.m. to 6 p.m.

The Museu Condes de Castro Guimarães (Condes de Castro Guimarães Museum) is a historical museum in the Old Torre de S. Sebastião that dates back to the early 1900s. At this museum, you can explore a collection of art, Indo-Portuguese furniture, a rare book collection, and ancient artifacts all left in the town of Cascais by Torre de S. Sebastião, a former Count of the house. The architecture is also worth exploring, especially the cloister in the museum's center, where you can view stunning Moorish-style tiles. This attraction is €5 per person to visit.

Boca do Inferno

If you're seeking an outdoor adventure, take a trip to Boca do Inferno, which translates to "Hell's Mouth." This dramatic cliff formation is in the Sintra-Cascais Natural Park, facing the Atlantic Ocean, where you can watch the waves crashing against the rocky cliffs.

The best time to see the water in its most violent action is when the surf is choppier when it can fill up the chamber. This spot is also a romantic area to come and watch the sunset with your partner. There is a viewing platform which gives perfect view of the Boca do Inferno.

You should also visit an excellent seafood restaurant Mar do Inferno and local handicraft market Mercandinho Boca do Inferno, selling regional memorabilas.

Museu do Farol de Santa Marta

Address: Avenida Rei Humberto II de Itália, Cascais 2750-800

Hours of operation: Tuesday to Friday from 10 a.m. to 6 p.m.

The Museu do Farol de Santa Marta (Santa Marta Lighthouse Museum) is an excellent opportunity to explore and learn about Portugal's maritime history. This lighthouse dates back to the 1860s and helped guide the ships in and out of the Tagus Estuary. If you choose to go to the museum, you will get to explore the lighthouse's interior, view artifacts, and see photos of the area throughout the years. There is also a documentary film you can watch giving an overview of the various lighthouses throughout Portugal. This attraction is €5 per person.

What to Do in Coimbra

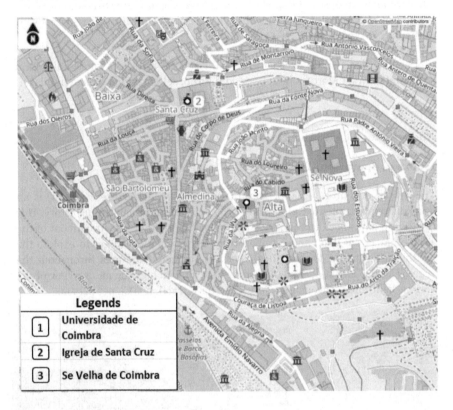

Universidade de Coimbra

Universidade de Coimbra (Coimbra University) has a couple of interesting historical pieces to it. One is that it is one of Europe's oldest schools in the country, as it was founded in 1290, but it is also only one of the five universities in the world to receive a UNESCO World Heritage Site accolade. While exploring the beautiful campus, I noticed some lovely architecture worth admiring and taking photos of. There will be different types of architecture from various periods, including Baroque, Gothic, and Neoclassical. The main highlight while visiting the university is the Joanina Library, which houses over 300,000 books. The Capela de São Miguel is another building to view on campus for its stunning ceiling and the Sala dos Capelos, which has portraits of Portugal's kings.

Igreja de Santa Cruz

Address: Praça 8 de Maio, Coimbra 3001-300

Hours of operation

- Monday to Saturday: 9:30 a.m. to 4:30 p.m.
- Sunday: 1 a.m. to 5 p.m.

The Igreja de Santa Cruz (Santa Cruz Monastery) is another ancient building that has existed since the 12th century. (Interestingly, the monastery was the reason the university was built and established.) You can explore the building and its stunning architecture at this monastery, including Portuguese Romanesque and Gothic styles with intricate carvings and stunning cloisters. You can also see the tombs, which serve as the final resting place for Portugal's first two kings. Admission into the cathedral attached to the monastery is free. Otherwise, it is €3 per person.

Sé Velha de Coimbra

Address: Largo da Sé Velha, Coimbra 3000-383

Hours of operation

- Monday to Friday: 10 a.m. to 5:30 p.m.
- Saturday: 10 a.m. to 6 p.m.
- Sunday: 11 a.m. to 5:30 p.m.

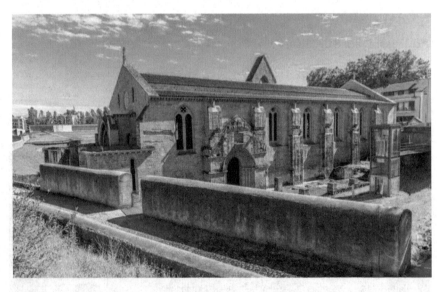

Sé Velha de Coimbra (Old Cathedral of Coimbra) is one of the most significant churches in Portugal as it was the first one built in Coimbra sometime in the late 1100s. Much of the architecture in the cathedral is still original as it didn't undergo many renovations throughout the years, giving you a raw look at some impressive Romanesque architecture. While here, it is worth taking some time to visit the cloisters, where you can find some peace. Inside the church, the main chapel is also fantastic to see. It dates back to the 16th century and was crafted from gilded wood.

There are also tombs you'll see throughout the cathedral. If you plan to visit Sé Velha de Coimbra, it costs €2.50 per person.

What to Do in Braga

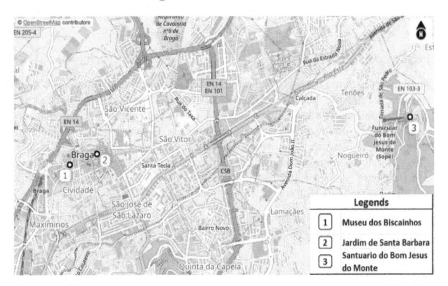

Museu dos Biscaínhos

Address: Rua dos Biscainhos, Braga 4700-415

Hours of operation

- The palace can be visited between 10 a.m. and 12:30 p.m. and 2 p.m. to 5:30 p.m.
- Between June and September, the gardens are open from 10 a.m. to 6:30 p.m.; from October to May, they are open between 10 a.m. and 12:20 p.m. and 2 p.m. to 5:20 p.m.
- The museum and gardens are closed on January 1, Easter Sunday, May 1, and December 25

The Museu dos Biscaínhos (Biscaínhos Museum) is a stunning former noble residence built between the 17th and 18th centuries. The building is gorgeous, and its Baroque architecture shows what life was like in that era. Inside the museum, you'll see furniture, tapestries, and beautiful porcelain reflecting the life of the elite throughout the mansion's rooms. You can also explore the gardens with lovely fountains, statues, and flowerbeds.

Ticket type	Price
Adults	€ 2
Seniors (65 years old and up)	€ 1
Children 12 years old and under	Free
Gardens	Free

Jardim de Santa Barbara

The Jardim de Santa Barbara (Santa Barbara Garden) is a lovely urban oasis if you want to escape the hustle and bustle of Braga. This garden is next to the Archbishop's Palace, a building dating back to the 14th century, giving visitors a medieval vibe with the arches from a former arcade. The garden itself was laid out in the 1950s following a Romantic style. The designer, Jose Cardoso da Silva, incorporated old statues, coats of arms, cornices, and a fountain with a statue of Santa Barbara (where the garden got its name). The garden is open all year round but is at its loveliest in the spring, summer, and autumn.

Santuario do Bom Jesus do Monte

The Santuario do Bom Jesus do Monte (Bom Jesus do Monte Sanctuary) is a UNESCO World Heritage Site and a significant pilgrimage destination dating back to the 14th century, with a staircase leading up to the church that took more than 400 years to complete. You'll notice that the stairs follow a zig-zag pattern, and on each landing, there are symbolic fountains, statues, and other Baroque-style decorations, along with various religious themes. If you intend to climb the stairs, it's 577 steps to the top, and you'll be rewarded with great views of Braga and its surroundings. However, if the steps aren't something you want to do, a funicular lift dating back to 1882 can bring you up. What is cool about this lift is that it operates with a counterbalanced water-weight system to bring you up to the top. The lift price is €3 per person for a round trip.

Once you are at the top, it is also worth exploring the church, which dates back to 1784. While the church is pretty bare and melancholy, there are some interesting religious paintings by Pedro Alexandrino to look at. The Museum of Confraria next to the church is also worth visiting, as it has several religious pieces on display and statues depicting Jesus's crucifixion.

Neighborhoods to Explore in Cascais, Coimbra, and Braga

Cascais

Old Town of Cascais

The Old Town of Cascais is the sleepy part of the city, offering a laid-back vibe for those who just want to stroll and take in the sights while blending in with the locals. As you wander around Cascais's Old Town, you will see many colorful and tiled adorned buildings on the streets—lovely squares like Largo Luís de Camões, where you'll find cafés serving delicious Portuguese pastries and coffee. As the sun sets for the day, walk along the waterfront promenade to admire beautiful views of the

Atlantic Ocean. You may even see some fishermen mending their nets before the following day's fishing.

Cidadela Art District

The Cidadela Art District is a great place for those who love exploring different art forms. In this neighborhood, people love to visit and admire artists at work and the six galleries in the area. If you keep your eyes peeled, you'll see plenty of street art and beautiful murals, too!

National Palace of Pena

Address: Estrada da Pena, 2710-609 Sintra, Portugal

The National Palace of Pena is 10.9 miles from Cascais. You can take the Line 1623 bus or Taxi from Cascais. The National Palace of Pena is an outstanding monument situated on the top of the Sintra Hills. The Palace and surrounding park trigger emotions of magnificence and sheer elegance. Traveller often gets lost in its charms.

The palace's colored tones symbolize Romanticism in Portugal. It's the best example of Ferdinand II's legacy as the King Artist, and it opens the doors to the imagination of all travelers. The surrounding park provides an idyllic scenario, frequently hidden under the mists that denote the

Sintra Hills. This has been the place of dreams for all the travelers who have passed here and gazed upon its magnificence.

Coimbra

Rua Ferreira Borges

Rua Ferreira Borges is one of Coimbra's main shopping streets, where you will find a diverse array of shops, cafés, and restaurants offering traditional Portuguese cuisine and sweets, as well as unique souvenirs. The street dates back to the Middle Ages and has not changed much in the past centuries. It's a nice place to take a walk and admire a different part of Coimbra, even if you're not intending to shop.

Braga

São Paio

While in Braga, it's worth visiting São Paio to appreciate the stunning architecture in the area. This neighborhood boasts large mansions and palaces dating back a few centuries, some of which you can look around, including the Museu Pio XII, which has several religious artifacts on display.

São Cristóvão

São Cristóvão is another great neighborhood to visit to explore great architecture. The streets are also lovely, which makes wandering a pleasant adventure. This neighborhood is also known for several great restaurants offering traditional Portuguese dishes.

Romantic Spots in Cascais, Coimbra, and Braga

Cascais

Eat at Bougain

If you're looking for a romantic dinner date, dine out at Bougain. They have a beautiful garden attached to the mansion and serve traditional Portuguese dishes. It's a romantic area to dine, celebrate your milestones as partners, and look forward to the rest of your trip.

Explore Guincho Beach

Guincho Beach is a picturesque stretch of coastline with dramatic cliffs and golden sands. It is a romantic haven for couples wanting to enjoy a beach day together. The beach is between the Atlantic Ocean and the Sintra-Cascais Natural Park, offering great views and perfect photo opportunities. If you and your partner are adventure-seeking, you may want to try water sports, such as surging, to add excitement to your adventure. This beach also boasts great sunset views if you want to walk in the evening around dusk.

Coimbra

Take a Wine Tour

Coimbra has many great wine tours you can research that lead just outside of Coimbra. A popular option is the Best Flavors of Winery Route, which allows you to take a full- or half-day journey through Portugal's wine country. This wine tour will teach you about Portuguese wine and the heritage of wine-making in Bairrada. You'll also visit wine cellars, taste wine, and take in the natural landscapes along the way. Depending on the tour you go on, you can expect

- a glass of champagne
- a driver and tour guide
- hotel pickup and drop-off
- admission to a few attractions, including Aliança Underground Museum, Caves Messias, and Caves do Solar de São Domingos.

If you take the half-day tour, the excursion will last around four hours, while the whole day is eight hours.

Sunset at Santa Clara Aqueduct

The Santa Clara Aqueduct dates back to the 18th century and was used as a water supply system for Coimbra, transporting water from the nearby Ave River. The towering arches that stretch across the landscape are beautiful, and if you and your partner arrive there around dusk, they are the perfect backdrop for watching the sunset! Remember to grab some wine and your camera to take great pictures as the sun casts a beautiful shadow on the arches.

Braga

Watch a concert at Theatro Circo

If you want to spend a romantic evening in Braga after dinner, see a show at Theatro Circo. This theater has many performances inside its stunning building, including fado performers.

Where to Eat in Cascais, Coimbra, and Braga

Cascais

Galeria House of Wonders

Address: 53 Rua da Misericórdia, Cascais 2750-642

Hours of operation: 8 a.m. to 11 p.m. daily
The Galeria House of Wonders is a lovely and affordable restaurant for vegetarians or vegans. Its great menu features salads, sandwiches, and more to satisfy any palette. Try to sit on its rooftop terrace, which offers excellent ocean views.

Baía do Peixe

Address: Av. Dom Carlos I 6, Cascais 2750-310

Hours of operation: 12 p.m. to 11:30 p.m. (closed on Mondays)
If you want to enjoy seafood while in Cascais, check out Baía do Peixe. This charming restaurant is located near Cascais's marina, so you'll have seafood and fish dishes with the freshest catches. They also have some great specials for sharing if you want to try a little of everything, which can help you save some money. Baía do Peixe can get quite busy, so make a reservation!

Coimbra

Refeitro da Baixa

Address: Quintal do Prior, Terreiro Erva Nºs 2 a 4, Coimbra 3000-339

Hours of operation: 12:30 p.m. to 3 p.m. and 7:30 p.m. to 10:30 p.m. (closed on Sundays)
Refeitro da Baixa is in a ceramic warehouse, creating a rustic atmosphere for your dining experience. At this establishment, you can expect a diverse range of Portuguese dishes, spanning from traditional to inventive creations of classic

dishes. They also have a great wine selection with many regional options to pair with your meal. The prices are also reasonable, making it easy to cater to any budget.

A Cozinha da Maria

Address: Rua das Azeiteiras 65, Coimbra 3000-116

Hours of operation: 11 a.m. to 3 p.m. and 7 p.m. to 11 p.m. (closed on Sundays)
A Cozinha da Maria is a cute little restaurant in downtown Coimbra serving traditional dishes from the region, including cod and the best goat stew (*chanfana*) you will ever taste. It comes out bubbling hot and loaded with meat in the tastiest broth. The prices are reasonable for the menu. However, ensure you bring cash, as they don't accept international credit cards.

Braga

Restaurante Retrokitchen

Address: 96 Rua do Anjo, Braga 4700-867

Hours of operation: 12 p.m. to 3 p.m. and 8 p.m. to 12 a.m. (closed on Tuesdays and Sundays)
Restaurante Retro kitchen is a great place to dine if you're seeking a laid-back ambiance. This establishment reminds many people of going to their grandparents' place with little objects that might take them back to their younger years as children, making them feel right at home as they feast upon some of their delicious dishes. Some of the best things to order here include duck magret, fish and shrimp *moqueca*, spinach soup, chicken curry, and salted caramel cheesecake.

Bira dos Namorados

Address: Rua Dom Gonçalo 85, Pereira, Braga 4700-032

Hours of operation
- Sunday to Thursday: 12 p.m. to 10:30 p.m.
- Friday and Saturday: 12 p.m. to 11 p.m.

Bira dos Namorados is a delicious burger establishment serving the best burgers in town. The burgers are cooked to perfection and served with tasty fries on the side. If you want to enjoy a beer with your burger, there is an excellent range of craft beers on the menu. This establishment also has a location in Porto.

What to Eat in Cascais, Coimbra, and Braga

Cataplana de Marisco

A seafood specialty, Cataplana de Marisco is a savory stew featuring a medley of seafood, such as prawns, fish, and crab, cooked with tomatoes, onions, and peppers in a traditional copper cataplana pot. This hearty and aromatic dish is a culinary highlight of Cascais, showcasing the region's rich maritime heritage.

Leitão à Bairrada

Coimbra's signature dish, Leitão à Bairrada, features succulent roast suckling pig seasoned with garlic, bay leaves, and white wine, slow-roasted until crispy on the outside and tender on the inside. Served with crispy skin and accompanied by orange slices, this dish is a flavorful and indulgent delight.

Chanfana

A traditional Portuguese dish, Chanfana is a hearty stew made with tender goat or lamb meat marinated in red wine, garlic, and spices, then slow-cooked until meltingly tender. Served with potatoes and accompanied by crusty bread, this rustic and flavorful dish is a favorite in Coimbra.

Cozido à Portuguesa

A hearty and satisfying meal, Cozido à Portuguesa is a traditional Portuguese stew featuring a variety of meats, such as beef, pork, and chicken, along with vegetables like potatoes, carrots, and cabbage, all simmered together until tender and flavorful. This comforting dish is a staple of Braga's cuisine, perfect for warming up on chilly days.

Rojões à Minhota

Rojões à Minhota is a traditional pork dish from the Minho region, featuring cubes of tender pork marinated in garlic, wine, and spices, then fried until crispy and golden. Served with potatoes and accompanied by pickled vegetables, this hearty and flavorful dish is a Braga classic.

Aletria

For dessert, Aletria is a creamy and comforting Portuguese dessert made with vermicelli pasta cooked in milk, sugar, and cinnamon until thick and creamy. Served chilled and garnished with cinnamon, this sweet and aromatic dessert is a delightful way to end a meal in Braga.

Bacalhau à Braga

Bacalhau à Braga is a delicious codfish dish that highlights the versatility of Portugal's favorite fish. Salted cod is cooked with potatoes, onions, and eggs, then baked until golden and topped with olives and parsley. This savory and satisfying dish is a Braga specialty, perfect for showcasing the region's culinary heritage.

Where to Stay in Cascais, Coimbra, and Braga

Cascais

Artsy Cascais

Address: Avenida Dom Carlos I 246, Cascais 2750-310

Artsy Cascais is a five-star accommodation by Ribeira Beach and Santa Marta Beach. This hotel has modern rooms in various sizes to suit your traveling needs. Some of the rooms have balconies or views of the ocean as well. If you choose to eat on-site, the restaurant offers international cuisine and can accommodate those who are vegan, vegetarian, or require dairy-free meals. Artsy Cascais can also rent a bicycle to explore the city without driving.

Estalagem Muchaxo Hotel

Address: Praia do Guincho, Cascais 2750-642

Estalagem Muchaxo Hotel is excellent if you want direct access to the beach. This accommodation is situated atop the cliffs overlooking the Atlantic Ocean. The rooms are cozy and simple, with some offering great views of the ocean—additionally, the outdoor pool backs into the ruins of a former fortress from the 17th century. The hotel also offers surfing and wind-surfing lessons if that is something on your bucket list.

Coimbra

Hotel Oslo

Address: Av. Fernao de Magalhaes, 25, Coimbra 3000-175

Hotel Oslo is a family-run accommodation offering stunning views of the city and Coimbra University. Staying at this hotel will give you easy access to several key attractions in Coimbra, including Sé Velha de Coimbra (Old Cathedral of

Coimbra). Several room options are available depending on if you're a couple traveling or are in Portugal with your family. Some rooms also have a balcony.

ArchiSuites

Address: 74 Avenida João das Regras, Primeiro Andar, Coimbra 3040-256

ArchiSuites is a modern and stylish accommodation in the heart of Coimbra, making it a convenient base from which to explore the city. Staying here puts you within walking distance of Coimbra's historical attractions, including the University and Sé Velha de Coimbra (Old Cathedral of Coimbra). Depending on your room type, you can choose to have a room with a balcony or one that overlooks the Mondego River.

Braga

Hotel Moon & Sun Braga

Address: Rua dos Capelistas 85, Braga 4700-307

Hotel Moon & Sun Braga is a four-star hotel in the city's heart. The rooms are sleek and stylish and equipped with the necessary amenities to make your stay comfortable. The hotel's convenient location makes it easy to access many of Braga's main attractions, including Museu dos Biscaínhos (Biscaínhos Museum).

The Arch

Address: Rua Dom Diogo de Sousa nº 51, Braga 4700-422

The Arch is located in Braga's historic old town, offering a comfortable self-catering option that is convenient for you. At this accommodation, you will find different apartment options equipped with a kitchenette and a terrace with a beautiful view of Braga. Staying here will put you within many of Braga's historical attractions, including Museu dos Biscaínhos (Biscaínhos Museum).

What Not to Do in Cascais, Coimbra, and Braga

Beware of Steep Terrain in Old Coimbra Town

It's best to explore Coimbra on foot, but old town areas in Coimbra have steep walking terrain. You can use an electric buggy to travel here. You can also rent out a bike or scooter to travel in Coimbra.

Don't Ignore Closing Time at Museu dos Biscaínhos

It will feel easy to get lost in the beautiful gardens of Museu dos Biscaínhos. However, remember that closing times are there for a reason, and the facility expects visitors to exit when the complex closes.

Don't Forget Good Walking Shoes for Santuario do Bom Jesus do Monte

If you plan to walk to the top of the steps at Santuario do Bom Jesus do Monte, make sure you're wearing good walking shoes! You don't want your feet to get sore.

Next Stop: The Algarve

Although Cascais, Coimbra, and Braga are in three parts of Portugal, each city has its unique cultural heritage worth exploring as you travel around the country. These cities are great stops along the way, allowing you to see the more remote parts of Portugal that you may not have considered visiting before.

In the next chapter, we will explore the famous Algarve coastline. This part of Portugal has stunning beauty and endless outdoor adventures. We'll explore some of the most romantic beaches to visit if you're planning this trip for you and your partner, as well as some great places to stay and eat. There is much more you have yet to see in Portugal!

Chapter 6:

The Algarve—Dos and Don'ts

The Algarve is one of the prettiest places in Portugal. It is built for adventure, from exploring the hidden coves and ruins to enjoying delicious Algarve cuisine throughout the picturesque area as you admire the coastline. Let's explore the lesser-known side of the Algarve, where each secluded beach and flavorful seafood meal will add a new chapter to your Portuguese travels.

Discovering the Algarve

The Algarve in Portugal is famed for its stunning coastline, vibrant culture, and sunny weather. It's the place people love to travel to when they want to soak up some vitamin D, swim in the Atlantic Ocean, and enjoy an array of outdoor activities. Beyond its beaches, the Algarve Region's history is richly displayed in its Moorish castles and charming towns like Lagos, Tavira, Faro, and Monchique. Naturally, if you're a big fan of seafood, this is one of the best places to feast, with many restaurants offering traditional dishes using fish and shellfish as their main ingredient. This is truly a haven for all sorts of travelers coming to Portugal to experience the sandy beaches, swim in the crystal clear waters of the Atlantic Ocean, hike along different trails, and explore the region's history. You'll soon find out why this part of Portugal remains a top choice for travelers from around the world!

Navigating the Algarve

The Algarve is a hot spot (literally and figuratively) for locals and tourists to flock to, especially during the summer when the weather is sunny. But of course, you can expect it to be busier during the peak season. So, again, it comes back to what type of traveler you are and whether you want to deal with more crowds or less crowds. If you want to experience fewer crowds, you're better off going to the Algarve in May or September when you're more likely to find accommodations (and it will be cheaper).

That being said, the Algarve isn't a tiny region in Portugal. Its coastline spans over 124 miles, and each area is significantly different. If you opt to go to the central part of the Algarve (Albufeira, Carvoeiro, Vilamoura, and Armação de Pêra), you can expect these towns to be the busiest (especially during the high travel season).

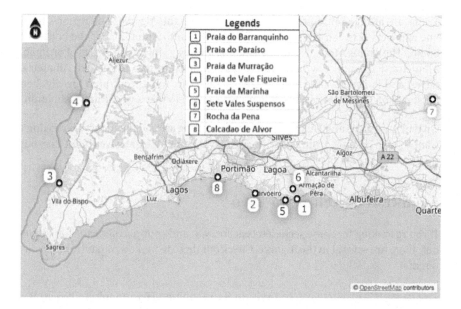

If you plan to go to the Algarve, try to stay in a small town along the western part of the Algarve. You'll be surprised by how the more secluded areas of this region (like Monchique, Porimão, and Praia da Rocha) will be less busy (even though they are resort towns).

Another thing you should do while visiting the Algarve is to rent a *toldo* (a canopy supported by wooden posts) to protect you from the sun. It's better than trying to lug around a rented beach umbrella, which can be awkward if you have a lot of stuff with you for your beach day. Again, if you are visiting the Algarve in the summer, you will want to book this in advance as it can be hard to secure.

As for getting around the Algarve, obviously one of the most convenient and fastest ways is by car. The two major roads connecting you to the various cities in the Algarve are the N125 and A22. (Remember to follow the road signs and drive on the right side if you're driving.)

Buses are another option in the Algarve but can be more complicated to plan even in the summer. Most bus companies in the area have limited departures (and even less on the weekends). However, if you plan to visit a famous beach or destination, you must take a bus if you're not driving. The bus companies in the Algarve that will offer you various destinations are Vamus (covering all of the Algarve), Próximo (servicing Faro and the surrounding region), Giro (servicing Albufeira), and Vai e Vem (covering Portimão).

Trains are also an option to take to travel through the Algarve. The region's train line connects between Laggos and Vila Real de Santo Antonió near the border of Spain. The trains stop in the towns along the way, including Silves, Portimão, Albufeira, Faro, and Tavria. If you're taking the train into towns like Albufeira, Silves, and Portimão, note that the train stations are not as central in the city. You must rely on taxis, Ubers, or public transportation to reach your final destination.

On that note, taxis and Ubers are options for getting around the Algarve if you don't want to take the bus, train, or drive. Taxis will be more expensive than Uber, but they are still a good option.

Secluded Beaches for Two

If you're looking for some secluded beaches, you and your partner can check them out; there are several in the Algarve. Check out these to make a romantic beach day out of it:

Praia do Barranquinho: Praia do Barranquinho (Barranquinho Beach) is a quaint beach near Porches nestled in a secret cove. This little slice of paradise has beautiful turquoise waters that are so clear that you can snorkel and watch the fish swimming around the rocks. To get to this beach, you will want to park near Albandeira Beach and then follow the path to your right while facing the water for five minutes.

Praia do Paraíso: Praia do Paraíso (Paradise Beach) is near the main beach in Cavoeiro down a long staircase. This beautiful, hidden beach has crystal clear waters, perfect for swimming and snorkeling. To get to this beach, there is parking near the Mar d'Fora restaurant, which also boasts excellent views of the cove.

Praia da Marinha: Praia da Marinha (Marinha Beach) is not too far from Lagoa and has some great coves to explore when the tide is out. This is one of the top beaches in Europe and Portugal, and surprisingly, it does not get flooded with people, making it a perfect secluded beach to enjoy with your partner.

Praia de Vale Figueira: If you and your partner are big nature lovers, you will want to go to Praia de Vale Figueira (Vale Figueira Beach) near Aljezur. This beach boasts natural beauty with stunning views from the cliffs or below. If you plan to visit this beach, wear good shoes, as the hike down is narrow and unpaved.

Praia da Murração: Praia da Murração (Murração Beach) is one of the most unspoiled secret beaches in the Algarve. Its beautiful turquoise waters, with gentle waves washing up onto the shore, make it a perfect spot to relax with a book or swim. This beach is close to the Costa Vicentina (an excellent place to go for a mountain bike ride).

Romantic Coastal Walks

Walking through the Algarve is a great way to enjoy the beautiful views of the area, see birds and other wildlife, and find quaint towns and historical spots that wouldn't normally make a travel guide. For you and your partner, this is a way to connect, challenge each other, and take in the magic and enchanting atmosphere of your trip. Consider adding one of these walks to your itinerary while in the Algarve.

Sete Vales Suspensos

The Sete Vales Suspensos (Seven Hanging Valleys) trail is a stunning hike that follows the western coastline of the Algarve between Praia da Marinha and Praia de Vale Centianes beaches. This easy-to-moderate trail boasts breathtaking views of the Atlantic Ocean and coves.

You can access the trailhead from either beach, and the roundtrip is around seven miles (so it takes about four to five hours in total). Depending on which trailhead you start at, the route will follow Praia da Marinha to Praia de Benagil, Alfanzina Lighthouse, and Carvalho Beach to Praia de Vale Centianes (and vice versa). However, starting at Praia da Marinha is better because there will be more free parking if you drive.

If you and your partner plan to hike this trail, it's best to do it in the spring or fall when the temperature is mild and there is less chance of rain. You'll also get some of the best photos, and it won't be as crowded with other people, making the hike more romantic.

Trilha Masmorra

The Trilha Masmorra (Masmorra Trail) is a circular hike near the Serra do Caldeirão. The round trip is a little over three miles and includes plenty of stunning scenery and views. One of the highlights is the Anta Masmorra burial site, which dates back between 3000 and 2001 B.C.E.

If you plan to hike this trail, it can be difficult, as it has many hills. If you're not great with hot weather, walking it in the spring or fall is better. Spring is also ideal due to the blooming flowers, citrus, and lavender. To access this hike, you'll find a well-posted sign and trailhead along the EN397 and EN124 that leads to Mealha.

Fonte Benémola

The Fonte Benémola (Benémola Fountain) trail is a rustic walk near Loulé with meadows, woodland, and farms. This circular walk should take about 90 minutes if you don't stop along the way. Its tranquil setting is romantic, bringing you to old kilns, ancient waterwheels, watermills, and freshwater springs. This area is also an excellent spot for you and your partner to spot several types of fish, including kingfishers and herons. Visiting this area in the spring is the best time for the flowers to bloom.

To access Fonte Benémola, the entrance is near Querença off EN124. Look for the well-posted sign. There is also a large parking area in the shade right at the start of the trail.

Rocha da Pena

Rocha da Pena (Pena Rock) is slightly more inland between Serra and Barrocal in the Algarve. This circular hike is around four miles and takes up to three hours to complete. If you and your partner are avid hikers, this will be a great way to challenge each other as you'll be climbing some steep rocks to the top of Rocha da Pena. From the top, you'll be rewarded with stunning views. While on this hike, you won't want to miss the stone battlements from the Iron Age. As you continue, you'll come across Penina, a small village where you can take a break and get something to eat.

As this is one of the most challenging hikes you can do, you will want to ensure you're wearing proper footwear to ensure your safety. The best place to start this hike is at the bottom of the Rocha da Pena. Also, keep an eye on your route markings, as it is easy to get distracted by the view and scenery.

Calçadão de Alvor

Calçadão de Alvor (Alvor Boardwalk) is a great romantic walk at any time of the year. The boardwalk begins near the harbor in Alvor and will take you along some of the wetlands and lagoons, offering beautiful views. This is a wonderful walk for nature lovers, especially when migrating birds make their way to this spot in the spring and fall.

If you walk along this pathway on a Sunday, stop by the market near the harbor to pick up fresh produce from local farms.

O Caminho Histórico

O Caminho Histórico (The Historical Way) is one of the longest trails you and your partner can follow. Spanning 143 miles, you can follow the trail that pilgrims once followed. This hike is broken up into 12 sections, allowing you to take a few days to follow the path. If you plan to do the entire hike (which will take up to six days), you will want to begin your hike in Santiago do Cacém near Setúbal, ending in Cabo de São Vincente. You'll see many historical sites along the way, including the Castle and Church of Santiago do Cacém. You'll also pass plenty of woodland and rural farm areas and see other flora and fauna.

Where to Eat in the Algarve

Sandbanks

Address: The Praca, Vale do Lobo, 8135-854 Almancil

Hours of operation
- Breakfast: 9:30 a.m. to 11:15 a.m., Lunch: 12 p.m. to 4 p.m., Dinner: 6:30 p.m. to 10:30 p.m.

Sandbanks is a restaurant in the Algarve Triangle, situated along the Vale do Lobo Beach, which offers excellent views of the Atlantic Ocean while you dine. At this establishment, you'll find a few different menus depending on the time of day you go, whether you're looking for a light breakfast or lunch or if you and your partner want to enjoy a romantic dinner. On this menu, you can expect a variety of grilled fish, shellfish, and vegan or vegetarian options; every dish is made to order.

Maria Petisca

Address: Rua José Afonso 12B, 8600-601 Lagos

Hours of operation
- Tuesday to Friday: 12 p.m. to 3 p.m. and 6 p.m. to 11:30 p.m.
- Saturday: 12 p.m. to 3 p.m. and 6 p.m. to 10:30 p.m.
- Sunday: 12 p.m. to 3 p.m.
- Closed on Mondays

Maria Petisca is all about eating small snacks, also known as *petiscos*. This surprisingly small restaurant is outside Lagos's old town and is a popular place among the locals, especially because the prices are cheap and the food is delicious. The menu features various pesticos crafted from locally sourced ingredients, including fresh seafood, tender meats, and in-season vegetables, all made to share.

A Charette

Address: Rua Dr.Samora Gil 30/34, Monchique 8550-461

Hours of operation
- Monday, Wednesday, and Thursday: 12 p.m. to 3 p.m. and 7 p.m. to 10 p.m.
- Tuesday, Friday, and Sunday: 12 p.m. to 3 p.m. and 7 p.m. to 11:30 p.m.
- Saturday: 12 p.m. to 3 p.m. and 7 p.m. to 11 p.m.

If you want a change of scenery from the beautiful coastlines, head toward Monchique, a quaint Portuguese mountain town. In this town, you'll find A Charette, a restaurant renowned for its authentic Algarve mountain cuisine. You can expect hearty dishes made with ingredients like boar and lamb if you eat here. However, one of the most popular choices is *codizo*, a traditional boiled dinner.

Taberna da Maré

Address: Travessa da Barca 9, Portimao 8500-755

Hours of operation:
12 p.m. to 3 p.m. and 6: 30 p.m. to 10:30 p.m. (closed on Mondays and Tuesdays)

One thing that you should try while visiting the Algarve is *cataplana*. This is the Algarve's way of cooking seafood: putting it in a giant clam-shaped copper pot with vegetables, potatoes, and broth to steam it all together while it cooks. As such, Taberna da Maré is one of the best restaurants in Portimao to try this succulent seafood dish. If you plan to try this restaurant, make reservations, as it can get quite busy.

Marisqueira Rui

Address: Rua Comendador Vilarinho Nº27, Silves 8300-128

Hours of operation:
12 p.m. to 4 p.m. and 6 p.m. to 11 p.m. Marisqueira Rui is closed on Mondays and Tuesdays from October to May and on Tuesdays from June to September.

If you are venturing to the town of Silves, Marisqueira Rui is a well-known seafood restaurant. This establishment is popular among locals and tourists who want to enjoy fresh seafood dishes. As such, you can expect various options, including grilled fish and shellfish specialties like prawns, clams, and lobster.

What to Eat in the Algarve

Cataplana de Porco

A hearty pork stew, Cataplana de Porco features tender chunks of pork cooked with onions, tomatoes, peppers, and herbs in a flavorful sauce. Served with crusty bread or rice, this comforting dish is a favorite among locals and visitors alike.

Cataplana de Marisco

A seafood lover's dream, Cataplana de Marisco is a flavorful stew made with an assortment of fresh seafood, such as clams, shrimp, and fish, cooked with onions, tomatoes, garlic, and herbs. Served in a traditional copper cataplana pot, this aromatic dish captures the essence of the Algarve's coastal cuisine.

Algarve Salad (Salada Algarvia)

A refreshing salad featuring crisp lettuce, tomatoes, onions, and peppers dressed with olive oil, vinegar, and herbs. Sometimes topped with olives and tuna, this simple yet flavorful salad is the perfect accompaniment to any meal in the Algarve.

Arroz de Polvo

A flavorful rice dish featuring a tender octopus cooked with rice, onions, tomatoes, and spices. The octopus is simmered until tender, infusing the rice with its rich flavor and creating a hearty and satisfying dish that is popular throughout the Algarve.

Bolinhos de Bacalhau

A beloved Portuguese snack, Bolinhos de Bacalhau are crispy, golden-fried codfish fritters made with salted cod, potatoes, onions, and parsley. Served hot and crispy, these savory bites are a popular appetizer or snack in the Algarve, perfect for enjoying with a cold drink by the beach.

Where to Stay in the Algarve

Casa dos Arcos

Address: 61 Rua 5 de Outubro, Albufeira Center, 8200-109 Albufeira

Casa dos Arcos is an affordable accommodation in Albufeira offering private and dorm rooms for your stay. This guest house is in a former 18th-century palace, and the rooms maintain some of their charm with a modern twist. This is a perfect base to stay in if you want to explore the old town and be close to the beaches.

Casa Apollo Guesthouse

Address: Rua Infante Dom Henrique 24, 8000-363 Faro

Faro is the town to be in if you want to enjoy the city life while exploring the Algarve. The Casa Apollo Guest House accommodation is in a late 19th-century house near Faro's city center, making it a perfect base to explore the city. The rooms are all comfortable (some overlook the outdoor pool), and you will get breakfast daily. Please note that this guesthouse is for adults only.

Rochavau Hotel

Address: Avenida São Lourenço da Barrosa, 8500-310 Portimão

Rochavau Hotel is a four-star family-run accommodation situated along Três Castelos Beach. This hotel is the perfect base if you plan to enjoy beach days. However, they also have an outdoor pool you can use. For your room type, you can choose one that has a balcony, terrace, or views of the Atlantic Ocean.

Three Marias Guest House B&B

Address: Rua Jogo da Bola nº8, 8600-717 Lagos

Three Marias Guest House B&B is a tranquil accommodation near downtown Lagos, making it an excellent base for exploring the main center, beaches, attractions, and restaurants. This guesthouse is quiet and perfect for travelers who want a place to chill after a day of exploring or spending time on the beach. All the room choices are double rooms, some with a private bathroom and others with a shared bathroom. Breakfast is served every morning. However, you are welcome to use the kitchen as well.

Calçada Guesthouse

Address: Calçada D.Ana 12, 8800-803 Tavira

Calçada Guesthouse in Tavira offers a blend of rustic charm and modern amenities. This hotel's location is an excellent base from which to explore Tavira's cultural attractions and is a short distance from the ferry docks to explore Tavira Island's beaches. The rooms in this guesthouse all have private bathrooms, with some overlooking the river.

What Not to Do in the Algarve

Don't Forget Sun Protection and Stay Hydrated

The Algarve Region can get hot in the summer, so don't forget to wear sunscreen (even on cloudy days)! The last thing you want to do is get a really bad sunburn. As such, you should also remember to stay hydrated to prevent sunstroke.

Look Out for a Red Flag

If you head to a beach and see a red flag, don't go into the water. The flag lets beachgoers know the water is unsafe due to rough seas or a strong current.

Don't Visit Overcrowded Beaches

As you research, you'll see many beaches that are recommended for you to visit, but many of these will be overcrowded! If you want a peaceful beach day, stick to some secluded beaches.

Check Pet Friendliness before going to beaches.

Some of the crowded beaches don't allow pets. Please check the pet-related regulations before visiting.

Don't Forget to Pack Food

If you are visiting some of the secluded beaches in the Algarve, planning and packing food and water is a good idea. Some of the beaches are not too close to restaurants, so you want to be prepared.

Don't Trespass Into Restricted Zones Along Hikes

There are a number of hiking trails in the Algarve. While following some hiking trails, you may come across wooden barriers that act as a restricted zone. Do not cross these for any reason. These wooden barriers protect the cliffs from further erosion.

Next Stop: Madeira and the Azores

As one of the most gorgeous places in Portugal, the Algarve has something for whatever type of traveler you and your partner are. This is one of the best areas to visit if you and your partner are outdoorsy. Even if you're not, there are plenty of secluded beaches where you can take in the sun and relax while listening to the ocean's waves.

If you are seeking more amazing adventures beyond the mainland, you may want to add Madeira and the Azores to your travel itinerary. These areas of Portugal have plenty of forests and volcanoes to explore, giving you more opportunities for travelers who are outdoor enthusiasts or for those wanting more tranquility within a beautiful natural setting.

Chapter 7:

Madeira and The Azores — Dos and Don'ts

U nlike other parts of Portugal, Madeira and the Azores add a different level of magic within their islands. If you've looked up pictures of Madeira and the Azores, picture yourself standing atop a misty peak as you gaze out to the Atlantic Ocean, spanning for miles or floating in the warm waters of the Azores. These Portuguese islands are not just another destination to add to your list. They offer countless opportunities for adventure with awe at every turn. What can you do in this part of Portugal? Let's find out.

Discovering Madeira and the Azores

Madeira and the Azores are two of the best archipelagos for travelers seeking outdoor adventure and surprises at every turn or want to slow down and embrace a few days of slower travel.

Madeira's four islands (Madeira, Porto Santo, Desertas, and Selvagens) are famous for their dramatic landscapes, dense forests, and rugged coastline. During your adventures here, you will see mist-covered mountains and cascading waterfalls that will create the perfect haven for you. As you explore the islands, you'll get to hike along paths that date back centuries, giving you a glimpse into Madeira's rich history. There is also an opportunity to learn about Madeira's influence in agriculture, with its temperature ideal for growing an array of fruits and vegetables, including sweet potatoes, oranges, guavas, pineapples, and bananas.

In contrast, the Azores comprise nine islands and present a sense of raw and untamed beauty. These islands are separated into three island groups: São Miguel, Santa Maria, and the Formigas islands in the east; Pico, Faial, São Jorge, Graciosa, and Terceira in the center; and Corvo and Flores in the northwest. Each island has distinct characteristics, including emerald-colored lakes in São Miguel and stunning tall cliffs in Flores. Visiting the Azores allows you to hike, watch for whales and dolphins, and dive. It also gives you a sense of tranquility if your goal is to soak up nature and relax.

Between Madeira and the Azores, you'll find many villages and towns steeped in rich history, showcasing more of where Portugal started and how the country has evolved through the centuries. Additionally, these archipelagos will leave a different imprint on your soul as you venture to their land, offering an escape from ordinary travel and a chance to find a new spark of adventure as you connect with nature.

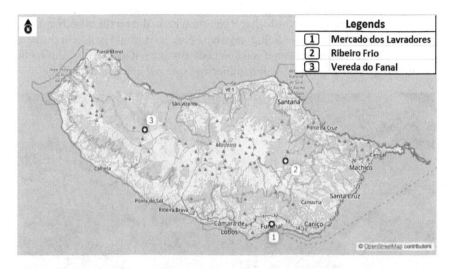

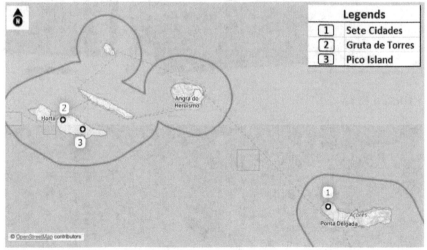

What to Do in Madeira and the Azores

Mercado dos Lavradores

Address: Mercado dos Lavradores, 9060-158 Funchal

Hours of operation: 7 a.m. to 7 p.m. daily

The Mercado dos Lavradores (Farmer's Market) is a beautiful market inside of a beautiful building dating back to the 1940s. Inside, you'll find the market is vibrant in color, with various fruits, vegetables, and flower vendors selling their goods. Prices for fruit are known to be higher if you shop here. But on the other hand, you may find exotic fruit you won't find anywhere else, so it would be worth the euro just to try something new. Even if you don't buy anything, it's a lovely way to spend the morning browsing the stalls and immersing yourself in the local heritage.

Ribeiro Frio

Ribeiro Frio is in the northern region of Madeira Island and is a haven for nature lovers and plant enthusiasts. In this park, surrounded by mountains, you'll find some easy hiking trails to follow without going on long hikes. Along the way, you'll see several plant species and rare birds, including the pigeon-trocaz (if you have a sharp eye, as this bird is the smallest on the island). There are great lookout points along the trails, making an excellent place to stop and drink water or have a light snack. (Remember that if you have any garbage, bring it when you leave!)

Sete Cidades on São Miguel Island

Sete Cidades on São Miguel Island is an outdoor adventurer's haven and an excellent first glimpse into the Azores' stunning landscape. This area is meant for adventure and offers impressive views of the iconic Green and Blue Lake and fantastic hiking trails.

If you want to take in epic panoramas, hike Miradouro do Cerrado das Freiras or Miradouro da Vista. If you go along Miradouro da Vista do Rei, the trail will bring you to the western side of the caldera and toward the little village. On the other hand, if you follow the Miradouro do Cerrado das Freiras trail, it will take you to the eastern side and lead you down to the village; this is the longest trail of the two. Regardless of which trail you decide to follow, you'll be rewarded with stunning views of the forests, lakes, and wildflower fields (if it's warmer). In addition to hiking, there are opportunities to stand-up paddleboard or kayak. These can be rented from the village at the bottom of the caldera.

Gruta de Torres

Address: Caminho da Gruta das Torres Criação Velha, 9950-000 Madalena

Hours of operation
- November 1 to March 31: 9 a.m. to 12:30 p.m. and 1:30 p.m. to 5 p.m. (closed on Mondays, January 1, and December 25).
- April 1 to October 31: 9 a.m. to 12:30 p.m. and 1:30 p.m. to 6 p.m. daily

This might not be something you will do every day: Explore a lava tunnel! At Gruta de Torres (Torres Cave), you will find the largest lava tube in Portugal. This tunnel is over 16,896 feet long and is estimated to be about 1,500 years old! During this excursion, you'll explore the first 1,450 feet with a guide while learning about the different geological formations and types of lava that make up the tube. This is a very unique experience and one worth doing! The tours are around 90 minutes and can be booked at the following times:

- November 1 to March 31: 9:30 a.m., 11 a.m., 2 p.m., 3:30 p.m.
- April 1 to October 31: 9:30 a.m., 11 a.m., 2 p.m., 3:30 p.m., 4 p.m.

Ticket type	Price
Adult (15 to 64 years old)	€ 10
Junior (7 to 14 years old) and senior (65 and up)	€ 5
Children 6 and under	Free

Romantic Adventures in Madeira and the Azores

Hike Vereda do Fanal

Vereda do Fanal is one of the most enchanting hikes on Madeira Island. Along this 11-mile hike (in one direction), you'll immerse yourself in a natural world, with a trail leading you through Laurisilva Forest, a UNESCO World Heritage Site. You'll gain fantastic views of Rabacal Valley, climb strenuous stairs, and finish in the magical Fanal Forest. Your hike will bring you through many misty-covered valleys and moss-covered forests as the birds sing their songs high up in the trees.

When you arrive in the Fanal Forest, thousands of ancient laurel trees tower over you. The branches of these stunning trees twist and tangle with one another, making you feel like you have stepped into a fairytale book. It is one of the most incredible hikes you and your partner can do on Madeira Island.

Pico Island: Full-Day Wine Culture Tour

One of the best romantic excursions you and your partner can take is a full-day wine culture tour on Pico Island in the Azores. On this eight-hour tour with Get Your Guide, you and your partner can embark on a guided tour through the stunning wine landscape of Pico, learn about the winemaking processes, and enjoy tasting different wines.

São Miguel Guided Tours

If you want someone to take care of your itinerary for you and your partner, check out some guided tours that will take you around São Miguel. On one of the tours with Get Your Guide, you, your partner, and your tour group will have the opportunity to explore a couple of plantations, including Gorreana Tea Plantation and Ponta Delgada's pineapple plantations, along with soaking in the hot springs in Furnas giving you and your partner a chance to connect with nature and enjoy the therapeutic waters. These tours typically last a full day, including pickup and drop-off at your accommodation.

Get Your Guide also offers a tour that will take you on a quad bike adventure through the rugged trails of São Miguel. On this excursion, your guide will take you to the 36,000-year-old Volcano of Seven Cities and other great spots with excellent viewpoints around the island. This excursion is about four hours long.

Azores: Private Tour Sete Cidades Green and Blue Lakes

On this excursion, you, your partner, and your tour group will be taken along San Miguel Island's west coast to explore the renowned volcanic crater of Sete Cidades and the Green and Blue Lakes. The journey toward Sete Cidades will also be a fun adventure for you and your significant other as the tour will take you by Pico do Carvão, where there will be an opportunity to take in the panoramic view and photos of the region with the Mountains Fogo and Vara in the distance. There will also be opportunities to explore some historical sites, including São Nicolau church. This tour is four hours long and includes pick up and drop off from your accommodation.

Where to Eat in Madeira and the Azores

Santa Maria Restaurante

Address: Rua de Santa Maria, 145, 9060-291 Funchal

Hours of operation: 12 p.m. to 11 p.m. daily

Santa Maria Restaurante is a popular establishment in Funchal on Madeira Island. At this eatery, you'll find a range of dishes to enjoy, including sushi, pasta, and risotto, all made with market-fresh ingredients. This restaurant also serves vegan options. Patrons love the atmosphere of eating at Santa Maria Restaurante. Although the restaurant is on Santa Maria Street, there is a lovely garden to sit in and enjoy your meal, taking you away from the hustle and bustle.

Uva Restaurant & Wine Bar

Address: Rua Dos Aranhas 27 - A, Se, 9000-044 Funchal

Hours of operation: 7 p.m. to 11:30 p.m. (closed on Sundays and Mondays)

Uva Restaurant & Wine Bar is a rooftop establishment at The Vine Hotel. You will get great panoramic views of the Atlantic Ocean and Funchal City at this restaurant as you dine on delicious dishes. You can expect various dish options bursting with multiple flavors and textures. The dishes are all nicely presented when they are served as well. While the prices aren't cheap, it is worth it for a romantic evening out, especially if you are staying at Hotel the Vine.

Estalagem da Ponta do Sol Restaurante

Address: Quinta da Rochinha nº6, 9360-529 Ponta do Sol

Estalagem da Ponta do Sol Restaurante is another fantastic restaurant boasting stunning views of the Atlantic Ocean. This restaurant is attached to the Ponta do Sol Inn and offers a mix of Mediterranean and European dishes. The prices are a bit higher, but it is worth it for the quality and service you'll get. The hours are not listed on the website, so if you stay at the hotel, you'll need to ask the concierge.

The Gardener Bar and Terrace

Address: Rua Padre Jose Jacinto Botelho 5, Furnas, Povoacao, São Miguel 9675-061

Hours of operation: 10:30 a.m. to 12 a.m. daily

The Gardener Bar and Terrace is part of the Terra Nostra Hotel and is situated in the garden. This establishment offers a versatile menu featuring tapas and other light eats. The prices are cheap, which is great if you're trying to stick to a budget. You'll love dining in the laid-back ambiance.

Captain's Table d'Angra

Address: Rua da Rocha, 14, Angra do Heroismo, Terceira 9700-144

Hours of operation: 12 p.m. to 2 p.m. and 6 p.m. to 11 p.m. (closed Sundays and Mondays)

Captain's Table d'Angra is an excellent restaurant for a fusion of flavors inspired by Portuguese, Greek, Italian, and Turkish cuisine. It offers a range of seafood and other delicious eats, whether you're there for something light or a full meal. The prices are budget-friendly, and some options can be served family-style.

Azores Wine Company—Restaurant

Address: Rua do Poco Velho, Bandeiras, Pico 9950-054

Hours of operation: 2 p.m. to 6 p.m. daily

Azores Wine Company—Restaurant may be the most expensive option, but one that will be a romantic one to do with your partner. At this establishment, you'll be able to enjoy a gastronomic experience where you and other guests sit at a communal table overlooking the Atlantic Ocean and enjoy a tasting menu with up to seven wines:

1. **In My Place:** The In My Place experience involves a six-course menu paired with four glasses of wine by the glass. It costs €120 per person.
2. **A Kind of Magic:** A Kind of Magic will take you on a culinary journey as you enjoy a six-course meal paired with five wines by the glass from Pico Island. This experience is €145 per person.
3. **Islands:** During the Islands experience, you will enjoy seven courses paired with six glasses of wine from Portugal, Spain, and Italy. This experience is €195 per person.
4. **Today is the Greatest Day:** This is one of Azores Wine Company's most unique menus. In addition to seven courses, you'll taste seven glasses of wine, some of the best wines from the Azores and Portugal. This experience is the most expensive, costing €375 per person.

If you do not drink, the restaurant can accommodate you and still offer a six- or seven-course meal. The six-course meal is €95 per person, and the seven is €120 per person.

If you plan to enjoy this, it's best to ensure you have a taxi to take you back!

What to Eat in Madeira and the Azores

Espetada

A traditional Madeiran dish, espetada consists of skewered and grilled chunks of marinated beef, typically seasoned with garlic, bay leaves, and coarse salt. Served on a laurel skewer, this succulent and flavorful meat dish is often accompanied by fried cornmeal or sweet potatoes, providing a satisfying taste of Madeira's culinary heritage.

Lapas Grelhadas

A popular dish in the Azores, lapas grelhadas are grilled limpets seasoned with garlic, lemon juice, and olive oil. These small shellfish are abundant in the Azorean waters and are enjoyed for their tender texture and briny flavor. Served hot off the grill, lapas grelhadas have a delicious taste in the Azores' coastal cuisine.

Queijadas da Graciosa

A specialty of the island of Graciosa in the Azores, queijadas da Graciosa are small cheese tarts made with local cow's milk cheese, sugar, eggs, and cinnamon. Baked until golden and slightly caramelized, these sweet and creamy tarts are a delicious dessert or snack enjoyed by locals and visitors alike.

Caldeirada de Peixe

A traditional fish stew popular in both Madeira and the Azores, caldeirada de peixe features a variety of locally caught fish, such as grouper, snapper, and mackerel, simmered with onions, tomatoes, peppers, and potatoes in a flavorful broth. Served piping hot with crusty bread, this hearty and aromatic stew is a favorite among seafood lovers.

Bifana

A classic Portuguese sandwich, bifana is made with thinly sliced marinated pork loin served on a crusty bread roll. The pork is typically seasoned with garlic, paprika, and white wine vinegar, then grilled or pan-fried until tender and flavorful. Served hot and juicy, bifana is a popular street food enjoyed throughout Madeira and the Azores.

Polvo à Lagareiro

A popular seafood dish in both Madeira and the Azores, polvo à lagareiro features a tender octopus cooked with garlic, olive oil, and herbs until tender and caramelized. Served with roasted potatoes and drizzled with more olive oil, this flavorful dish showcases the fresh seafood and vibrant flavors of the islands.

Carne de Vinha d'Alhos

A traditional dish from Madeira, carne de vinha d'alhos is a flavorful marinated pork dish made with wine, garlic, and spices such as cloves, cinnamon, and bay leaves. The pork is marinated overnight to allow the flavors to develop, then slow-cooked until tender and succulent. Served with rice and fried potatoes, this dish is a beloved part of Madeiran cuisine.

Cozido das Furnas

A traditional Azorean dish, cozido das Furnas is a hearty stew cooked in the natural geothermal heat of the Furnas volcanic area. Made with a variety of meats, such as beef, pork, and chicken, as well as vegetables and sausages, this flavorful stew is slowly cooked underground for several hours, resulting in tender meat and vegetables infused with smoky volcanic flavors.

Bolo do Caco

A staple of Madeiran cuisine, bolo do caco is a round, soft, and slightly sweet bread made with sweet potato and cooked on a hot stone slab. Served warm with garlic butter or as a sandwich filled with grilled meats or seafood, this iconic bread is a must-try in Madeira.

Where to Stay in Madeira and the Azores

The Vine Hotel

Address: Rua Dos Aranhas 27 - A, Se, 9000-044 Funchal

The Vine Hotel is a five-star accommodation that is well-loved for its stunning rooms overlooking Madeira's beautiful landscape. At this adult-only hotel, you'll find large rooms fitted with soaker tubs and blackout curtains; some have a seating area in addition to the comfy bed. The Vine Hotel also has an outdoor pool, hot tub, and sauna. If you want to enjoy a beach day, the Almirante Reis Beach is the closest to the accommodation, and you can rent sun loungers and umbrellas.

Hotel Madeira

Address: Rua Ivens, Nº21, Sé, 9000-046 Funchal

Hotel Madeira is an excellent choice for travelers seeking a hotel that offers comfort and is close to the adventure. This three-star hotel has spacious rooms with great ocean views or Funchal views. Beyond the rooms, you'll find an outdoor swimming pool with sun loungers, a rooftop bar, and spa services. This is the perfect hotel to choose if you and your partner want to stick to a budget without losing all the luxury.

Ponta do Sol Inn

Address: Quinta da Rochinha nº6, 9360-529 Ponta do Sol

Perched atop a cliff facing the Atlantic Ocean, Ponta do Sol is a converted farmhouse with breathtaking ocean views that offer a lovely and romantic retreat within the island's natural beauty. The rooms boast bright furnishings and have views of the sea or the garden. A tennis court is also on site if you and your partner want to play a round. Additionally, Ponta do Sol has a spa where you can take advantage of massage services and a Turkish bath. Ponta do Sol is about 50 meters from the hotel for beach days.

Azoris Angra Garden—Plaza Hotel

Address: Praça Velha, 9700-201 Angra do Heroísmo

Azores Angra Garden—Plaza Hotel is in the UNESCO World Heritage Site and historical town of Angra do Heroísmo. Though this is a four-star hotel, it is affordable and has many amenities that will make your stay pleasant. At Azoris Angra Garden—Plaza Hotel, you can use a pool and spa service. It is also a little over 800 feet from the Zona Balnear da Prainha Beach, where you can rent beach chairs to enjoy a beach day.

Atlantida Mar Hotel

Address: Boavista, n 9, 9760-557 Praia da Vitória

Atlantida Mar Hotel is a four-star hotel in Praia da Vitória. It offers a range of amenities, including a pool and fitness center and rooms with balconies offering views of the ocean or the mountain. This hotel is an ideal base for those who want to be near several outdoor action areas and three beaches. The hotel can also help arrange car rentals to make exploring the surrounding area easier.

Hostel da Palmeira

Address: Rua da Lapa nº7, 9760-484 Praia da Vitória

Hostel da Palmeira is the cheapest accommodation option if you are a traveler seeking a simple place to stay without frills. You'll find your room choices at this hostel between single rooms or dormitories and a shared lounge, kitchen, and terrace. Some rooms also have balconies, and others have views of the ocean.

What Not to Do in Madeira and the Azores

Don't Forget to Bring a Jacket

While Madeira and the Azores tend to be the warmest parts of Portugal and see plenty of sunny days, it doesn't mean it won't rain or get cool in the evenings. While checking the weather before your departure date is always wise, pack a jacket anyway. You never know if you might need it!

Don't Wear Flip-Flops on Pebble Beaches

If you are heading to a beach with pebbles, be warned that they can be slippery, making exiting the ocean a challenge. If you have water shoes or something else that can stay on your feet, wear those to give you traction and protect your feet from the black sand, which will get very hot in the sun.

Don't Trust Google Maps Entirely

In Madeira, some roads are for pedestrians only. At certain intersections, one leg of the road is open for vehicle traffic, and the other leg is only for pedestrians. Please check road signages for directions along with Google Maps.

Don't Be Afraid to Ask Locals

Sometimes, we feel lost or turned around—it happens! The locals are friendly and can help you find your way. If you're concerned about a language barrier, you'll find many of the locals speak English.

Next Stop: Guimarães, Santarém, and Faro

Madeira and the Azores are the two best places for outdoor adventure, so there will be no shortage of things to do. From immersing yourself in the daily lives of the locals shopping at the Mercado dos Lavradores Farmer's Market to exploring the Gruta de Torres (Torres Cave), these two archipelagos will leave lasting memories when you return home. As you plan your trip, consider what adventures, restaurants, and accommodations stood out from this chapter and what you want to add to your itinerary.

Moving away from the oceanic adventures and stunning landscapes of Madeira and the Azores, we will be venturing to Guimarães, Santarém, and Faro. You'll find lesser-known towns rich with history and cultural heritage along the cobblestones. This is where Portugal's world began, and it's an opportunity to glimpse into the heart and soul of this magnificent country.

Chapter 8:

Guimaraes, Santarem, and Faro—Dos and Don'ts

G uimarães, Sanatrém, and Faro each have unique qualities where you can wander cobblestoned streets and find history hidden within the walls. In these three towns that go from north to south, you'll be able to experience medieval architecture and history and uncover the heart and soul of Portugal. There are many adventures to be had. What more could you ask for on this epic trip to Portugal?

Discovering Guimarães, Santarém, and Faro

This quaint Portuguese town is situated in the northern part of Portugal and is where you will get to see some fantastic architecture from the medieval era and even before that time. Of course, one of the most important landmarks in Guimarães is the Guimarães Castle, offering superb city views and a glimpse into Guimarães's rich history. Also mesmerizing and on the same property as the castle is the Ducal Palace, or Paço dos Ducques de Brangança, where you'll find lovely gardens adding to the grandness of this historic building. For other ways to glimpse into Guimaraes's history, the city's center is listed as a UNESCO World Heritage Site. You'll find plenty of lovely squares, ancient churches, and other architecture that will take you back to an older era and way of life.

In Sanatrém, you'll be more in the center of Portugal, filled with history and stunning architecture. Among its landmarks that allow you to glimpse into the city's history, you'll want to explore areas like Igreja de Santa Clara (Santa Clara Church) and the historic city center. Beyond the attractions and exploring the city center, this region has plenty of parks that allow you to take in other landscape views, opening the door for more adventure.

Faro, the capital of the Algarve, is a stunning old town with plenty of beaches and a dynamic cultural setting. While we covered the beaches in the Algarve in Chapter 5, exploring Faro will allow you to explore Gothic architecture and more, especially if you visit the Sé Catedral de Faro. You'll also find that the city center is filled with notable parts from the city's history, including medieval walls along alleys and whitewashed buildings adorned with colorful tiles. Faro is a great city to visit, especially if you see the Algarve. It will open the door for outdoor adventure, especially at the Parque Natural da Ria Formosa (Ria Formosa Natural Park).

You will find several things to do as you explore these areas in Portugal, whether in the north, middle, or southern section. The nice thing about visiting any of these towns is that it's easy just to wander. Make a small itinerary, but let your adventurous soul lead beyond that. When you stop looking, you truly see some of the beauty.

What to Do in Guimarães

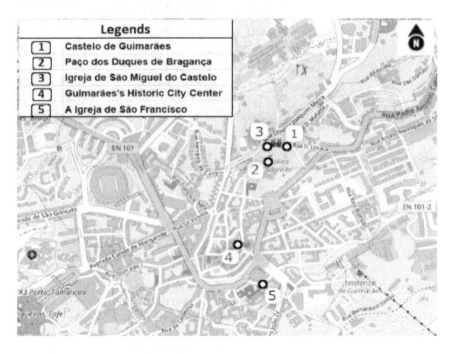

Castelo de Guimarães, Paço dos Duques de Bragança, and Igreja de São Miguel do Castelo

Address: Rua Conde Dom Henrique 3, 4800-412 Guimarães

Hours of operation: 10 a.m. to 6 p.m. daily (last admission is at 5:30 p.m.)
With Guimarães being where Portugal began, your trip should include visiting the iconic Guimarães Castle, the Ducal Palace, and the Church of São Miguel to understand Portuguese history better.

Castelo de Guimarães (Guimarães Castle) was built in the 10th century on the order of the Countess of Portugal, D. Mumadona Dias, as a place of refuge when invaders landed in the country from the sea. With its placement atop the hill, the church also allowed guards to keep watch of the surrounding countryside, making the castle an ideal defensive stronghold for impending attacks.

Throughout its history, Guimarães Castle has seen several key events, including the Battle of São Mamede in 1128 and the Battle of Ourique in 1139 as led and conquered by King Alfonso Henriques I. These historic victories, especially with the Battle of São Mamede, helped lay the foundation for Portugal as a country. Inside the castle, you'll see its former life and impressive architecture.

Adjacent to the castle is the Paço dos Duques de Bragança (Ducal Palace), built in the 15th century under the direction of D. Afonso de Barcelos, the first Duke of Bragança. Eventually, the residence fell into disrepair but was restored in 1937 and completed in 1959. A museum is housed inside the Ducal Palace, where you can see artwork, furniture from the 17th century, weapons, and tapestries that tell the story of the Portuguese arriving in Arzila.

Lastly, the Igreja de São Miguel do Castelo (Church of São Miguel is a small church dating back to the 13th century. Featuring Romanesque architecture, the church is a simple chapel and serves as the final resting place for the warriors from Portugal's founding years beneath the floor.

Together, these three monuments serve as reminders of Guimarães important history to Portugal. It is a beautiful way to spend a morning or afternoon exploring the timeless charm and get an understanding of where this beautiful country began.

Ticket type	Ducal Palace only	Guimarães Castle only	Both
Adults (25 to 64 years old)	€ 5	€ 2	€ 6
Youth (13 to 24 years old) and Seniors (65 and up)	€ 2.50	€ 1	€ 3

Visiting the Church of São Miguel is free.

Explore Guimarães's Historic City Center

Guimarães's Historical City Center is renowned for its medieval architecture and other architectural details that point to various periods in Portugal's rich history. As such, take the time to follow the cobblestoned streets *without* an agenda. This is an excellent opportunity to see some of the most iconic squares, including Largo da Oliveira, where you'll find several historical buildings along with the Church of Nossa Senhora da Oliveira, a 10th-century church with stunning arches and columns in the interior. You'll also see many charming medieval-era homes, archways connecting houses, and other statues. Don't forget to ensure your camera and phone are charged because you'll surely take tons of photos!

A Igreja de São Francisco

Address: Rua Padre Gaspar Roriz, Igreja de São Francisco, Guimarães 4810-429

Hours of operation
- Tuesday to Saturday: 9:30 a.m. to 12 p.m. and 3 p.m. to 5 p.m.
- Sunday: 9:30 a.m. to 1 p.m.
- Closed on Mondays

The A Igreja de São Francisco (Church of San Francisco) is a little outside Guimãres's city center and is renowned for its beautiful interior and garden. Initially constructed in the 1400s and later renovated in the 18th century, the Church of San Francisco has stunning tile work depicting St. Anthony's life, elaborate stone carvings, and a wooden roof displaying an illusion painting. This church is a free attraction to visit.

What to Do in Santarém

A Igreja de Santa Clara

Address: Avenida Gago Coutinho e Sacadura Cabral, 2005-021 Santarém

Hours of operation
- Tuesday: 2 p.m. to 6 p.m.
- Wednesday: 9:30 a.m. to 12:30 p.m. and 2 p.m. to 6 p.m.
- Thursday to Sunday: 9:30 a.m. to 12:30 p.m. and 2 p.m. to 6 p.m.
- Closed on Mondays

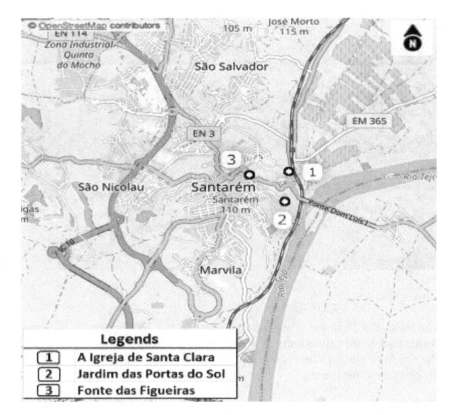

The A Igreja de Santa Clara (Church of Santa Clara) is a 13th-century church outside Santarém's city limits. Constructed for D. Lenor Alfonso III's daughter, the church is another excellent example of Gothic architecture on the outside. However, it underwent renovations, which changed the interior. The upgrades were considered controversial as they reshaped the inside of the church, losing its artistic history and other valuable information about how the church developed throughout the different generations. Nonetheless, you'll see some stunning stone carvings, elegant carvings, towering spires, and a rose window that bathes the inside of the church in beautiful sunlight. Admission to this church is free.

Jardim das Portas do Sol

The Jardim das Portas do Sol (Garden of Portas do Sol) is a beautiful space atop a hill near Santarém's city center. Here, you can enjoy a picnic, take a stroll, and see breathtaking views of the surrounding countryside, including the Tagus River. This is a peaceful retreat to enjoy while you explore Santarém.

Fonte das Figueiras

The Fonte das Figueiras (Fountain of Figueiras) is a hidden gem in Santarém dating back to the 14th century. It is a restful spot to stop by if you're arriving in the city from Almeirim and is one of the few remaining examples of Gothic civil architecture in the country.

The fountain is a simple structure with pyramid-shaped merlons that blend against the walls of the São Salvador parish. At the time of its construction, the fountain was where locals would gather and use the water to wash their clothes. It is a peaceful area to explore and has an enchanting atmosphere with the surrounding trees.

What to Do in Faro

Sé Catedral de Faro

Address: Largo da Sé 11, 8000-138 Faro

Hours of operation
- Monday to Friday: 10 a.m. to 6:30 p.m. daily (closes at 6 p.m. in December and January)
- Saturday: 9:30 a.m. to 1 p.m.
- Closed on Sundays

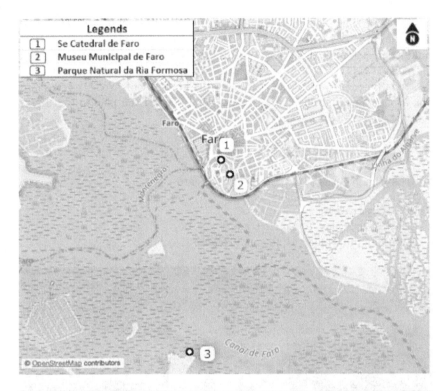

Legends
1 Se Catedral de Faro
2 Museu Municipal de Faro
3 Parque Natural da Ria Formosa

Sé Catedral de Faro (Faro Cathedral) is a stunning Faro church boasting several architectural styles, including Romanesque, Gothic, and Baroque. While the outside is intriguing, with its different carvings and the bell tower standing tall above the church's surroundings, the inside will leave you in awe. The church has multiple chapels with their characteristics. Stunning altarpieces, paintings, and gilded woodwork create a tranquil and sacred atmosphere. You also don't want to miss the 18th-century pipe organ painted with Chinese motifs. You can get a closer look at it if you climb the stairs to the second floor. If you plan to visit the Sé Catedral de Faro, it is €3.50 per person.

Museu Municipal de Faro

Address: Largo Afonso III, nº 14, 8000-167 Faro

Hours of operation
- Tuesday to Friday: 10 a.m. to 6 p.m.
- Saturday and Sunday: 11:30 a.m. to 6 p.m.

Surprisingly, Faro, while not very big, has several museums to explore. However, the Museu Municipal de Faro (Municipal Museum of Faro) is worth visiting as it is situated inside an old convent building and features some of the most impressive archeological exhibits. One of the must-see areas in the museum is the Mosaic of Oceanus, which dates back to around the second or third century. This well-preserved mosaic was discovered when the train station was being built in 1926. If you plan to visit this museum, admission is €2 per person.

Parque Natural da Ria Formosa

For outdoor enthusiasts, you will want to visit the Parque Natural da Ria Formosa (Ria Formosa Natural Park), which stretches nearly 40 miles along the Algarve's coastline. There are over 44,400 acres of land to explore by taking a boat tour, biking, hiking, kayaking, or paddleboarding. In this park, you'll find a diverse species of birds, including greater flamingos, spoonbills, little terns, oystercatchers, white storks, and herons. In addition to birdwatching, there are opportunities to explore the flora and fauna in the park, including many species of fish, crustaceans, and marine mammals. There are also several beaches with golden sand and crystal-clear waters if you want to dip your toes in and cool off. This is a must-visit destination for anyone wishing to explore the Algarve region and take in its many opportunities.

Where to Eat in Guimarães, Santarém, and Faro

Guimarães

Tasquinha do Tio Julio

Address: Rua de Couros 20, 4810-225 Guimarães

Hours of operation: 12 p.m. to 2 a.m. (closed on Sundays)

Tasquinha do Tio Julio has been in business since 1981. Serving kebabs and delicious soups, this is a wonderful restaurant to eat at if you're looking for a quick bite. It is a highly-rated establishment, and everyone who has eaten here has rated it. The prices are also relatively cheap, with food costing around €5 to €10 per person.

Adega do Ermitão

Address: Rua da Penha, 4810-041 Guimarães

Hours of operation: 12:30 p.m. to 9 p.m. daily

Adega do Ermitão is one of the most unique experiences you can have while in Guimarães. This restaurant is situated in Monte da Penha's forest, where you can enjoy your meal in a canteen made of boulders and rocks. This establishment is cheap, and you can enjoy flatbreads, sardines, savory pastries called *rissois*, and ribs. If you eat here, remember to bring cash as they don't take cards.

Santarém

Ó Balcão

Address: Rua Pedro de Santarém 73, Santarém, 2000-223

Hours of operation: 12 p.m. to 3 p.m. and 7 p.m. to 11 p.m.

Ó Balcão is a lovely restaurant if you and your partner want to enjoy a romantic dinner. This establishment serves plenty of fish and seafood locally sourced from the chef's home region in the Ribatejo province. Duck, boar, and other meats are also on the menu for enjoyment. When you enter the restaurant, you and your partner will feel like you have entered a tavern, with the tiles on the walls adding a romantic atmosphere.

O Pizzas de Santarém

Address: Praceta Cónego Dr. Manuel Nunes Formigão 7B, 2005-256 Santarém

Hours of operation: 11 a.m. to 3 p.m. and 6 p.m. to 10 p.m.

O Pizzas de Santarém is an excellent and affordable option for those who crave pizza instead of traditional Portuguese dishes. At this establishment, you'll find various pizza options made with the freshest ingredients and cooked in a wood-fired oven. This restaurant provides a casual dining atmosphere, and you can expect prompt service.

Faro

Vó Bela

Address: Rua do Alportel 271, 8005-334 Faro

Hours of operation
- Tuesday to Saturday: 12 p.m. to 4 p.m. and 7 p.m. to 11 p.m.
- Sunday: 12 p.m. to 4 p.m.
- Closed on Mondays

Vó Bela is well-known for its authentic Portuguese cuisine and generous servings. You and your partner can dine on traditional dishes in the cozy atmosphere, including hearty stews and flavorful meat, fish, and seafood. This restaurant sources ingredients from local vendors to ensure the perfect quality for every dish they make.

Taberna Zé-Zé

Address: Travessa do Alportel 15, 8000-448 Faro

Hours of operation: 6 p.m. to 11 p.m. (closed on Sundays)
Taberna Zé-Zé is a popular option among tourists and locals looking to enjoy authentic Portuguese cuisine in a relaxed atmosphere. At Taberna Zé-Zé, you'll find a great menu featuring seafood, grilled fish, and other meat specialties sourced from the area. In addition to the different menu options, they offer some dishes designed for two people to make sharing easy and affordable.

What to Eat in Guimarães, Santarém, and Faro

Pica-pau

A traditional dish from Guimaraes, pica-pau features tender cubes of beef or pork sautéed with garlic, olive oil, and spicy peppers. The meat is cooked until golden brown and served with crusty bread for dipping, making it a flavorful and satisfying appetizer or main course.

Sopa da Pedra

Originating from Santarem, sopa da pedra is a hearty and flavorful bean soup made with a variety of beans, smoked meats, and vegetables. The soup is cooked slowly until the flavors meld together, and a hot stone is added to the pot to enhance the richness of the broth. Served piping hot with crusty bread, sopa da pedra is a comforting and delicious meal enjoyed throughout the region.

Açorda de Marisco

Another popular seafood dish from Santarem, açorda de marisco, is a hearty bread soup made with a variety of shellfish, such as clams, mussels, and shrimp, cooked in a flavorful broth with garlic, onions, and tomatoes. The soup is thickened with bread and eggs, giving it a creamy texture and rich flavor. Served hot with a drizzle of olive oil and fresh cilantro, açorda de marisco is a delicious and comforting meal that is perfect for warming up on a chilly day.

Carne de Porco à Alentejana

A traditional pork dish from Faro, carne de porco à alentejana features tender cubes of pork marinated in garlic, paprika, and white wine vinegar, then sautéed with onions and seasoned with fresh herbs. The pork is then simmered with clams in a savory broth until tender and flavorful. Served hot with crusty bread or rice, carne de porco à alentejana is a delicious and satisfying meal that highlights the flavors of the Alentejo region.

Amêijoas à Bulhão Pato

A classic Portuguese seafood dish from Guimaraes, amêijoas à bulhão pato features tender clams cooked in a flavorful broth made with garlic, olive oil, and fresh herbs, such as cilantro and parsley. The clams are cooked until they open and release their briny juices, infusing the broth with their rich flavor. Served hot with crusty bread for dipping, amêijoas à bulhão pato is a delicious and satisfying appetizer or main course.

Queijo da Serra

A famous cheese from the Serra da Estrela region near Santarem, queijo da serra is a creamy and flavorful sheep's milk cheese that is aged for several months to develop its rich flavor and creamy texture. The cheese is typically served at room temperature with crusty bread or fruit preserves, allowing its complex flavors to shine. Creamy, tangy, and slightly nutty, queijo da serra is a delicious and indulgent treat that is perfect for cheese.

Where to Stay Guimarães, Santarém, and Faro

Guimarães

Pousada Mosteiro de Guimarães

Address: Largo Domingos Leite de Castro, Lugar da Costa, 4810-011 Guimarães

Pousada Mosteiro de Guimarães is set in a monastery that dates back to the 12th century when it was under the direction of Queen Malfalda. The building once served as a monastery, so you'll find several historical references.

The rooms have heated wooden floors decorated with beautiful rugs and period furniture. The on-site restaurant is not to be missed. It's in the old wine cellar with gorgeous archways, and one of their best dishes is the monkfish with rice, clams, coriander, and prawns.

Casa do Ribeiro

Address: Selho São Cristovão, 4810-316 Guimarães

Casa do Ribeiro will be one of the most unique options to stay in if you are headed to Guimarães. The building dates back to the 17th century and is still owned by the later generation of the family who first built the house. It's almost like you'll be staying in a museum in addition to finding a comfortable stay. There are even photos of the family around the house you can see, as well as beautifully landscaped gardens to explore.

As this accommodation is a bed and breakfast, you can expect to start your day with a hearty meal. As for attractions nearby, the Guimarés Castle is about three miles away, and the city center is about a 15-minute drive from the accommodation. This is an excellent option for travelers who want to find a quaint place to stay, and prices are about mid-range.

Santarém

Casa do Alfaro

Address: Quinta do Alfaro Norte Estrada do Alfaro, 2050-361 Azambuja

If you want to stay just outside Santarém's city center, Casa do Alfaro is about 30 minutes away and is an affordable option. This beautiful hotel has stunning views and an outdoor pool in a vast green space. It is a good option for travelers visiting Portugal with their families as it has family rooms. Breakfast is also included with your room fee to start your day.

Santarém Hotel

Address: Avenida Madre Andaluz, 2000-210 Santarém

The Santarém Hotel is a centrally located accommodation in the city's heart. This affordable accommodation offers standard amenities, including some rooms offering panoramic views of Santarém. This hotel will be within walking distance of several attractions, including the Gardens of Portas do Sol.

Faro

Chapter 6 also features another accommodation option if you will be in Faro. Otherwise, this is a fantastic alternative, especially for those looking for romantic retreats!

Hotel Faro and Beach Club

Address: Praça Dom Francisco Gomes 2, 8000-168 Faro

Hotel Faro and Beach Club is the ultimate romantic retreat to check out while in Faro. This hotel is ideally situated near Faro's city center and has its own beach you can enjoy. This hotel also has a stunning terrace pool boasting incredible ocean views. There are also spa services you can take advantage of.

Next Stop: Exploring the Heart of Portugal

Guimarães, Santarém, and Faro may have been the lesser-known towns on your radar until you read this chapter. We have gone through many things you can do in these parts of Portugal. While they are widely separated, consider them as stops to wherever else you plan to go in this beautiful country.

In the upcoming chapter, we'll explore everything that makes up the heart of Portugal. The center has plenty of rural charm and more adventures to be had. From exploring the Schist Villages to following the Bela Trail to finding some tremendous romantic retreats, you'll be guaranteed opportunities to ignite your soul for travel or connect deeper with your partner as you take in the beautiful landscapes of Portugal.

Chapter 9:

The Heart of Portugal—Dos and Don'ts

Beyond Portugal's vibrant cities lies many areas destined for adventurous souls wanting to see the rural areas where living a slower life is the norm. Outside the bustling towns, you'll find quaint villages with a rich past, vineyards stretching to the horizon, and dense forests that are a haven for outdoor enthusiasts. This chapter is about what you can do in Portugal's countryside, where romance can blossom in the adventures and cultural experiences you can have.

Going off the Beaten Path

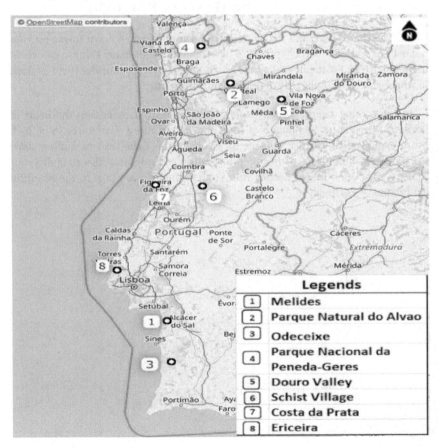

Legends

1	Melides
2	Parque Natural do Alvao
3	Odeceixe
4	Parque Nacional da Peneda-Geres
5	Douro Valley
6	Schist Village
7	Costa da Prata
8	Ericeira

Portugal's countryside can lead to some epic areas filled with adventure and places to explore quaint towns and adventure in national parks. Check out some of these ideas that you and your partner can do for other trips around Portugal:

Melides: Melides is a small beach town along the stunning Alentejo coast where you can find some of the best beaches in Portugal. Visiting this town is perfect for those who want to have a relaxing few days in Portugal between the bigger cities or the crowds in the Algarve. Because this town is not busy, exploring it is a treat because you won't find an influx of tourists, allowing you to see Portuguese daily life authentically.

Parque Natural do Alvão: Parque Natural do Alvão (Alvão Natural Park) is one of the best places to go to if you and your partner love finding outdoor adventure. The rugged mountain range of Serra surrounds this natural park do Alvão, offering great views of the surrounding landscape. This park is also home to the famous Fisgas do Ermelo waterfall, over 650 feet tall. You will also likely encounter wildlife in the park, including adorable otters swimming in the river, mountain goats grazing on grass, and more. You'll also find small villages scattered throughout, including Lamas de Olo, characterized by stone buildings.

Odeceixe: Odeceixe is a cute cobblestone beach village with white-washed buildings near several beaches, including the Praia de Odeceixe. At this beach, you will find perfect water for snorkeling, soft sands to laze on, and rugged cliffs to create a beautiful background. There are opportunities to kayak or paddleboard, and the beach is near the Rio de Seixe River, which leads to the sea. When you're done adventuring around the beach or exploring it from the water, check out the village, where you will find some great shops and cafés.

Parque Nacional da Peneda-Gerês:

Parque Nacional da Peneda-Gerês (Peneda-Gerês National Park) is the only national park in Portugal with stunning mountains, rivers with clear water, valleys, and cascading waterfalls. It is one of the best places for any outdoor enthusiast, with so much to see and do while following the hiking paths that range in difficulty. If you and your partner aren't up for hiking, you can rent canoes or kayaks to explore the park from the rivers or try your hand at mountain biking. You'll also find ancient landmarks here, including the Castelo de Lindoso (Lindoso Castle), which is rich with history, and the stone-housed village of Fafião, a former hunting town. Whichever way you plan to spend the day in this park, there is plenty of room to make it romantic with your partner.

Douro Valley: Douro Valley is an excellent romantic retreat off the beaten path with many vineyards to explore. The valley is a short train ride from Porto if you stay in that town. Some of the top vineyards to visit include Quinta de La Rosa, Quinta da Roêda, and Quinta do Panascal for their rustic settings and beautiful views of the Douro Valley as you taste the different wine blends.

Schist Villages: Schist Villages is one of the best romantic destinations you can take. This area comprises 27 little villages grouped together with buildings created from schist stone. When you approach the villages, it will feel like it is frozen in time, and wandering around the streets will create this comforting atmosphere with many opportunities to see how the locals live their rural lives. As the houses are perfectly set in with the natural landscape, many boast incredible views of the surrounding area. For example, if you go to Casal de São Simão in the mountains of Serra da Lousã, you'll get great views of the Zêzere River. If you're an art fan, you'll want to check out Cerdeira, where you can see several art galleries with local art. Go to this area without an agenda. You'll be surprised by what you and your partner find!

Costa da Prata: You will want to go to Costa da Prata for more romantic beach retreats. This area also has some incredible rock formations that will increase the awe compared to the Algarve. If you head to Peniche, it has a dramatic coastline leading to pristine beaches. If you and your partner are surfers, test yourselves by going to the beaches in Nazaré, which have amazing waves to surf. When you're ready to pack up your beach excursion, head to the UNESCO World Heritage Site, Óbidos, between Porto and Lisbon. This town has plenty of architecture, quaint restaurants, and more to discover. (P.S. Óbidos is a great village to visit around Christmas when it is decked out for holidays! Are you swooning yet?)

Ericeira: If you are a surfer, Ericeira is another great place to go in the heart of Portugal. If the sport is on your and your partner's bucket list, aim to visit Ericeira between April and October, when the water is much calmer. Additionally, the town is a romantic area where you'll find many unique shops, cafés, and restaurants with delicious seafood dishes.

Romantic Hiking Trails and Romantic Ruins

Hiking is always a wonderful way to connect with each other and nature. There is something romantic about wandering through the wilderness, finding beautiful rivers and waterfalls, and simply just being with one another. On the other hand, exploring some ancient ruins is also a romantic excursion as you and your partner get to learn about the people who came before our time:

Blue Well Route: The Blue Well Route is a 5.2-mile round-trip hike in the Braga District near the town of Termas do Gerês. As you hike the rugged terrain, this route will challenge you and your partner. It will bring you to the blue well with a small waterfall. There are also some great viewpoints along the way. This hike will take around 2.5 hours, depending on how fast you go.

Caminhos do Pão e Caminhos da Fé: Caminhos do Pão e Caminhos da Fé is in the Peneda-Grês National Park and is about three miles, round trip. This hike is challenging (and sometimes slippery) but will bring you to some incredible viewpoints and past waterfalls. You may also encounter some cows that roam freely in the area.

Fafião Viewpoint and Green Well Trail: The Fafião Viewpoint and Green Well Trail is a shorter trail that is about 1.92 miles as a roundtrip. Along this beautiful hike, you will find an easy route, bringing incredible viewpoints of the mountains and surrounding landscape. Some hikers on this trail say the way back is challenging but fun!

Roman Ruins of Conímbriga: Viaje Portugal is a tour company operating out of Coimbra that will take you on a four-hour tour to explore the Roman ruins of Conímbriga. It is one of the most important historical monuments in Portugal, where you'll see excavated Roman houses, tiles, columns, and ancient thermal baths. You'll also be taken to the Conímbriga Monographic Museum to see more Roman artifacts on display.

More Romantic Retreats

If you and your partner want some other romantic retreat ideas where you can spend a couple of days relaxing, check out these accommodations.

Pedras Salgadas Spa and Nature Park

Address: Parque de Pedras Salgadas, 5450-140 Pedras Salgadas

Staying at Pedras Salgadas Spa and Nature Park allows you to enjoy a self-catering bungalow in the woods of Parque de Pedras Salgadas (Pedras Salgadas Park). The beautiful surroundings will allow you and your partner to connect as you relax in your temporary home equipped with a living area and a fully equipped kitchen. If you don't feel like cooking, no worries! They also have a restaurant where you can eat or order from your room. You and your partner can enjoy several treatments and massages in the spa. They also have a steam room, hot spring bath, and sauna you can use. This is the perfect area to relax for a few days if you want to do nothing.

Ecorkhotel Evora

Address: Quinta da Deserta e Malina, 7000-804 Évora

Situated in Évora in the Alentejo region, Ecorkhotel is the perfect romantic retreat for couples who want to enjoy the pool or go on adventures in the nearby forests. This hotel also has a large wellness center where you and your partner can enjoy various services, including couples massages.

Tipi Algarve

Address: There are two locations available. They are

1. Monte Joao Afonso, 8501-911
2. Alameda Algarve, 8400-020 Estômbar

If you and your partner want to camp instead of staying in a traditional accommodation, check out Tipi Algarve. Technically, you'd be glamping in a canopied tent with a proper bed. However, the campsite is a beautiful retreat where you can relax in the woods with a book or be close to several beaches in the Algarve. Additionally, this accommodation offers other wellness services, including massages, guided meditation, and yoga.

Areias do Seixo Villas

Address: Praceta do Atlântico, Mexilhoeira, Póvoa de Penafirme, 2560-046 Santa Cruz

Areias do Seixo Villas offers beautiful villas where you and your partner can relax and take in the beauty of Portugal's Silver Coast. The villas have a rustic vibe and feature balconies with great views of the surrounding landscape. Additionally, the accommodation offers massages.

Portugal's Cultural Festivities and Holidays

In Chapter 1, we covered some of Portugal's cultural festivities to check out. Depending on when you plan to go to Portugal, you may want to consider checking out some of these other festivals and events that happen throughout the year:

Dia de Reis: Dia de Reis (also known as King's Day) takes place on January 6 and celebrates the end of Christmas. During this event, choirs sing Christmas-themed carols at the doors of Portuguese homes.

Dia da Assunção de Nossa Senhora: Dia da Assunção de Nossa Senhora (also known as The Feast of the Assumption of Mary or Assumption Day) is a religious holiday that occurs on August 15. This holy day commemorates the Virgin Mary's death and her assumption into heaven. Aside from mass in churches, some towns may hold other cultural events, so you will want to do some research ahead of time to see what else could be happening on that day.

Madeira Wine Festival: The Madeira Wine Festival is a fun event for those who love wine. This festival typically takes place at the end of August and into the early weeks of September, and attendees can taste wines from participating wineries, learn about their winemaking processes, and more!

Dia da Implantação da República: Dia da Implantação da República (also known as Republic Day) is an October holiday with significant historical significance. October 5 is the day that marked the end of the monarchy in Portugal in 1910 and the beginning of a new era of democracy and political change.

Your Great Adventure Starts Now!

The heart of Portugal has plenty of adventure and romance that can make up a perfect travel tale and memoir. In this chapter, we looked at several things you can do outside of Portugal's major cities and towns that will allow you to immerse yourself in other parts of Portugal that aren't overly touristy. By venturing to areas like the Schist Villages, where you can see many stone houses to immersing yourself in cultural festivals like the Madeira Wine Festival and finding ways to relax and unwind as a couple, your trip will be full of memories to share with your friends and family back home.

Conclusion

P ortugal is one of the most beautiful countries in the world and is worth visiting for romantics! Throughout this book, we explored the various parts of Portugal so that you can build an itinerary that will make your trip memorable. Beyond the attractions, you have learned about many hidden gems in Portugal, where you can glimpse into the rich history and learn about what makes Portugal's heartbeat.

In addition to exploring Portugal's various towns and major cities, you now know the different ways to get around. You also have a better idea of how to navigate Portugal's cultural etiquette so that you can feel confident in interacting with the locals.

From the various areas we have explored, now is the time to start thinking about when you want to go and how long you plan to be in Portugal. With so much to see and do, you likely won't see everything on your list, so it's time to go back and review the attractions that stood out. Of course, the absolute joy of travel will lie in the experiences you have and the memories you create while exploring. That said, don't use this book as your endpoint but as your starting point. When you allow your traveling soul to take some of the lead, you'll never know what experiences you'll immerse yourself in or what more you may encounter.

If this book has helped you start planning your trip to Portugal, please consider giving the gift of travel and adventure to someone else by providing a review on Amazon.

Glossary

- **Água:** Water
- **Beritivo:** Appetizer
- **Bebida:** Beverage or drink
- **Bom dia:** Good morning
- **Boa noite:** Good night or good evening
- **Boa tarde:** Good afternoon
- **Cerveja:** Beer
- **Com licença:** Excuse me
- **Como está?:** How are you?
- **Como faço para chegar até...:** How do I get to...
- **Desculpe, eu não entendo:** Sorry, I don't understand
- **Estou ben:** I'm good (in response to, "How are you?")
- **Estou pronto para fazer o pedido.:** I am ready to order.
- **Eu estou perdido:** I am lost
- **Eu gostaria de...:** I would like to...
  - alugar uma bicicleta (rent a bicycle).
  - comprar um ingresso (buy a ticket).
  - **Fala inglês?:** Do you speak English?
- **Frango:** Chicken
- **Fruta:** Fruit
- **Não:** No
- **Obrigada:** Thank you (if you are a female)
- **Obrigado:** Thank you (if you are a male)
- **Olá:** hello
- **Onde é... :** Where is:
  - banheiro (the restroom)?
    - a entrada (the entrance)?
  - ponto de ônibus (the bus stop)?
    - a estação de transporte público (the public transportation station)?
    - a estação de trem (the train station)?
- **Peixe:** Fish
- **Posso/podemos:** May I or may we
- **Praia:** Beach
- **Prato principal:** Main course
- **Por favor:** Please
- **Qual é o especial hoje?:** What is the special today?
- **Quanto custa isso?:** How much is this or how much does this cost?
- **Rua:** street
- **Posso pegar um café?:** May I get a coffee?
- **Salada:** Salad
- **Sim:** Yes
- **Vegetais:** Vegetables
- **Você pode me levar ao aeroporto?:** Can you take me to the airport?
- **Vinho:** Wine

References

Algarve. (n.d.). VisitPortugal. https://www.visitportugal.com/en/destinos/algarve

Algarve transportation guide. (n.d.). Algarve Portugal Tourism Guide. https://www.algarveportugaltourism.com/transportation

Alya. (2023, April 4). *The historical way of the Rota Vicentina - a 2023 guide*. Stingy Nomads. https://stingynomads.com/historical-way-rota-vicentina/#Day_1_Santiago_de_Cacem_%E2%80%93_Vale_Seco_185_km114_mi

Anna. (2022, January 30). *The most beautiful road trip in the Algarve*. To the Sea Stories. https://www.totheseastories.com/post/the-most-beautiful-road-trip-in-the-algarve

ArchiSuites. (n.d.). Booking.com. https://www.booking.com/hotel/pt/archisuites-coimbra.fr.html

Areias do Seixo Villas. (n.d.). Booking.com. https://www.booking.com/hotel/pt/areias-do-seixo.en-gb.html

Artsy Cascais. (n.d.). Booking.com. https://www.booking.com/hotel/pt/artsy-cascais-cascais.fr.html

Ashton, A. (2023, June 4). *Guide to port wine cellars in Porto*. Nomads Travel Guide. https://www.nomads-travel-guide.com/guide-to-port-wine-cellars-in-porto

Atlantida Mar hotel. (n.d.). Booking.com. https://www.booking.com/hotel/pt/atlantida-mar.en-gb.html

Azores: Private tour Sete Cidades Green & Blue Lakes. (n.d.). Get Your Guide. https://www.getyourguide.com/sao-miguel-island-l1663/azores-private-tour-sete-cidades-green-blue-lakes-t609772/?ranking_uuid=840f8625-357e-4f24-b25c-6c553c80e7ba

Azoris Angra Garden – Plaza Hotel. (n.d.). Booking.com. https://www.booking.com/hotel/pt/angra-garden.en-gb.html

Bairro do Avillez. (n.d.). Tripadvisor. https://www.tripadvisor.com.br/Restaurant_Review-g189158-d15613782-Reviews-Bairro_do_Avillez-Lisbon_Lisbon_District_Central_Portugal.html

Belém Tower in Lisbon. (n.d.). Civitatis Lisbon. https://www.lisbon.net/belem-tower

Bernhardt, P. (2020, June 8). *8 top-rated tourist attractions in Guimarães*. Planet Ware. https://www.planetware.com/tourist-attractions/guimaraes-p-bra-guim.html

Best activities for nature lovers in Madeira. (n.d.). Europe's Best Destinations. https://www.europeanbestdestinations.com/travel-guide/madeira/madeira-best-activities-for-nature-lovers

Best romantic getaway spots in Portugal. (2024, February 2). Portugal.com. https://www.portugal.com/activities-experiences/best-romantic-getaway-spots-in-portugal

Best things to do in Sintra for couples. (n.d.). Tripadvisor. https://www.tripadvisor.com/Attractions-g189164-Activities-zft12169-Sintra_Sintra_Municipality_Lisbon_District_Central_Portugal.html

Bira dos Namorados, Braga. (n.d.). Tripadvisor. https://www.tripadvisor.ca/Restaurant_Review-g189171-d7056433-Reviews-Bira_dos_Namorados_Braga-Braga_Braga_District_Northern_Portugal.html

Birtles, K. (2022, September 22). *15 basic Portuguese language phrases & words to know before you travel to Portugal*. The Real Word. https://www.trafalgar.com/real-word/basic-portuguese-phrases

Blue Well Route. (n.d.). AllTrails. https://www.alltrails.com/trail/portugal/braga/rota-do-poco-azul

Blyth, A. (2022, October 17). *The most charming neighbourhoods in Porto, Portugal*. Culture Trip. https://theculturetrip.com/europe/portugal/articles/the-5-most-charming-neighborhoods-in-porto

Bom Jesus do Monte. (n.d.). Atlas Obscura. https://www.atlasobscura.com/places/bom-jesus-do-monte

Book your tickets. (n.d.). Taylor Fladgate. https://www.taylor.pt/us/visit-taylor-fladgate/book-your-tickets

Braga neighborhoods. (2023, January 28). Travel Regrets. https://travelregrets.com/braga-neighborhoods

Braga, Portugal; A tourism, day trip, and holiday guide for 2024. (n.d.). Porto-North-Portugal.com. https://porto-north-portugal.com/braga-portugal-guide.html

Brett, S. (2024, April 4). *Walking the Seven Hanging Valleys Trail in Algarve, Portugal*. Moon & Honey Travel. https://www.moonhoneytravel.com/seven-hanging-valleys-trail-algarve-portugal

Bryan, L. (2017, December 4). *Driving in the Algarve, Portugal*. Downshiftology. https://downshiftology.com/driving-algarve-portugal

Buy. (n.d.). Metropolitano de Lisboa. https://www.metrolisboa.pt/en/buy

Calcada Guesthouse. (n.d.). Booking.com. https://www.booking.com/hotel/pt/calcada-guesthouse.fr.html

Captain's Table. (n.d.). Explore Terceira. https://www.exploreterceira.com/en/mapa-interativo-en/local/captains-table

Casa Apollo Guesthouse. (n.d.). Booking.com. https://www.booking.com/hotel/pt/casa-fialho.fr.html

Casa do Alfaro. (n.d.). Booking.com. https://www.booking.com/hotel/pt/casa-do-alfaro.en-gb.html

Casa do Infante in Porto. (n.d.). Civitatis Porto. https://www.introducingporto.com/casa-do-infante

Casa do Ribeiro. (n.d.). Booking.com. https://www.booking.com/hotel/pt/casa-do-ribeiro-guimaraes.en-gb.html

Casa dos Arcos – Charm Guesthouse. (n.d.). Booking.com. https://www.booking.com/hotel/pt/hostel-casa-dos-arcos.fr.html

Cascais, Portugal: A tourism guide for 2024. (n.d.). Cascais-Portugal.com. https://www.cascais-portugal.com

Cascais sightseeing guide. (n.d.). Cascais Portugal Tourism Guide. https://www.cascaisportugaltourism.com/guide

Castelo de Guimarães. (n.d.). VisitPortugal. https://www.visitportugal.com/en/node/134223

Chen, K. I. (2022, November 2). *Common Portuguese phrases and words for your next trip to Brazil or Portugal*. Travel + Leisure. https://www.travelandleisure.com/travel-tips/basic-portuguese-words-phrases-for-travel

Chilton, G. (2023, December 13). *74 must-know Portuguese words & phrases for beginners*. Preply. https://preply.com/en/blog/portuguese-words-phrases-for-beginners

Civitatis. (n.d.). *Conimbriga Roman ruins trip from Coimbra*. Civitatis. https://www.civitatis.com/en/coimbra/conimbriga-roman-ruins-trip

Coimbra, Portugal in 2024: An independant travel guide. (n.d.). MyPortugalHoliday.com. https://myportugalholiday.com/coimbra-portugal.html

Collins, C. (2018, August 26). *The 10 best stops to make on your road trip to the Algarve Coast*. Free Two Roam. https://www.freetworoam.com/2018/08/27/10-best-stops-algarve-coast

Concannon, E. (2024, January 24). *Is Algarve safe? Top safety tips for Algarve in 2024*. Emily Embarks. https://emilyembarks.com/is-algarve-safe

Crystal Palace Gardens. (n.d.). Local Porto. https://www.localporto.com/crystal-palace-gardens-porto

Date ideas in Braga. (n.d.). Boo. https://boo.world/hy/resources/date-ideas-in-braga

Date ideas in Coimbra. (n.d.). Boo. https://boo.world/resources/date-ideas-in-coimbra

Discover the rich history of the Belém Tower. (n.d.). Belem Tower Tickets. https://www.belemtowertickets.com/history

Dodsworth, L. (2020, March 11). *Exploring the Ribeira: getting lost in Porto Old Town*. On the Luce Travel Blog. https://www.ontheluce.com/getting-lost-in-portos-old-town

Ecorkhotel Evora. (n.d.). Booking.com. https://www.booking.com/pt/ecorkhotel-evora-suites-spa.en-gb.html

Editores da Time Out Lisboa. (2024, January 23). *10 romantic restaurants in Cascais*. Time Out. https://www.timeout.com/cascais/restaurants/romantic-restaurants-in-cascais

Estalagem Muchaxo Hotel. (n.d.). Booking.com. https://www.booking.com/hotel/pt/estalagem-muchaxo.pt-pt.html

Events and festivals in Portugal. (n.d.). Exoticca. https://www.exoticca.com/us/europe/western-europe/portugal/events

Excellence and authentic flavors. (n.d.). Terra Nostra Garden Hotel. https://www.bensaudehotels.com/en/terranostragardenhotel/tn-restaurant-the-gardener-bar-terrace

Exmo Hotel by Olivia. (n.d.). Booking.com. https://www.booking.com/hotel/pt/exmo.en.html

Faro Cathedral. (n.d.). Faro Portugal Tourism Guide. https://www.faroportugaltourism.com/guide/faro-cathedral.html

Faro Museum. (n.d.). Faro Portugal Tourism Guide. https://www.faroportugaltourism.com/guide/faro-archaeological-municipal-museum.html

Faro, Portugal: A tourism guide for 2024. (n.d.). Algarve-Tourist.com. https://www.algarve-tourist.com/Faro-portugal-guide.html

Five less known Lisbon neighborhoods to explore. (2015, July 13). Taste of Lisboa Food Tours. https://www.tasteoflisboa.com/blog/5-less-known-lisbon-neighborhoods/

Five of the best parks and gardens in Lisbon. (n.d.). The Hidden Secrets of Lisbon. https://www.the500hiddensecrets.com/portugal/lisbon/discover/parks-and-gardens

Fonte das Figueiras. (n.d.). VisitPortugal. https://www.visitportugal.com/en/NR/exeres/0CEDE938-F950-4140-AE3A-8062A18178C0

Fox, J. D. (n.d.). *Cool things to do in Guimaraes*. Julie Dawn Fox in Portugal. https://juliedawnfox.com/guimaraes

Frasca, M. (2024, January 17). *Best walks in the Algarve*. My Guide Algarve. https://www.myguidealgarve.com/travel-articles/best-walks-in-the-algarve

Frendo, D. (n.d.). *Lisbon for couples: Romantic activities & date night ideas*. Grumpy Camel. https://www.grumpycamel.com/romantic-things-to-do-in-lisbon

From Madeira to Mars. (2016, March 31). *16 do's and don'ts in Madeira*. https://frommadeiratomars.com/16-dos-and-donts-in-madeira

Furnas in São Miguel Island: The thermal hot spot of the Azores. (n.d.). Getaways Azores. https://azoresgetaways.com/en-ca/destination/azores/islands/sao-miguel/furnas-village

Furnas: Tea plantations, lake and volcano guided tour. (n.d.). Get Your Guide. https://www.getyourguide.com/furnas-l1726/furnas-east-island-nature-experience-t327871/?ranking_uuid=840f8625-357e-4f24-b25c-6c553c80e7ba

Getting around Portugal: Transportation tips. (n.d.). Rough Guides. https://www.roughguides.com/portugal/getting-around

Glamping UK. (n.d.). *Glamping in Portugal at Tipi Algarve*. https://www.glamping-uk.co.uk/Glamping-in-Portugal-at-Tipi-Algarve/Glamping-News

Globejour. (n.d.). *Portugal on a budget: Understanding the currency and 10 travel hacks*. https://globejour.com/portugal-on-a-budget-understanding-the-currency-and-10-travel-hacks

Gonzalo. (n.d.). *Portugal, more than 300 days of sunshine per year*. LisbonGuide. https://lisbonguide.org/portugal-more-than-300-days-of-sunshine-per-year

Gorlinski, V. (n.d.). Fado. In *Encyclopedia Britannica*. Retrieved April 1, 2024, from https://www.britannica.com/art/fado

Groves, J. (2023, June 25). *Vereda do Fanal hike (PR13) On Madeira Island*. Journey Era. https://www.journeyera.com/vereda-do-fanal

Gruta das Torres Visitors Centre. (n.d.). Governo Dos Açores. https://parquesnaturais.azores.gov.pt/en/parques/5/centro/8

Guided visits. (n.d.). Museu Do Fado. https://www.museudofado.pt/en/guided-visits-en

Guimarães. (n.d.). VisitPortugal. https://www.visitportugal.com/en/content/guimaraes

Hansen, M. (2024, March 26). *Where to stay in Porto: A complete guide for first timers*. Wheatless Wanderlust. https://wheatlesswanderlust.com/where-to-stay-in-porto

Historical overview. (n.d.). Santa Cruz. https://santacruz.ces.uc.pt/en/historical-overview

History. (n.d.). Museu Do Fado. https://www.museudofado.pt/en/history-en

History of Lisbon. (n.d.). Civitatis Lisbon. https://www.lisbon.net/history

Holyoake, S. (n.d.). *The top five secluded beaches on the Algarve*. Vintage Travel. https://www.vintagetravel.co.uk/blog/top-five-secluded-beaches-algarve

Hostel da Palmeira. (n.d.). Booking.com. https://www.booking.com/hotel/pt/hostel-da-palmeira.en-gb.html

Hotel Faro & Beach Club. (n.d.). The Hotel Guru. https://www.thehotelguru.com/hotel/hotel-faro-beach-club-faro

Hotel Madeira. (n.d.). Booking.com. https://www.booking.com/hotel/pt/madeira-funchal.pt-pt.html

Hotel Moon & Sun Braga. (n.d.). Booking.com. https://www.booking.com/hotel/pt/dos-terceiros.fr.html

Hotel Oslo. (n.d.). Booking.com. https://www.booking.com/hotel/pt/oslo.fr.html

House of Wonders. (n.d.). Happy Cow. https://www.happycow.net/reviews/house-of-wonders-cascais-45979

Igreja de Nossa Senhora da Oliveira - Guimarães. (n.d.). VisitPortugal. https://www.visitportugal.com/en/content/igreja-de-nossa-senhora-da-oliveira-guimaraes

Igreja de Santa Clara - Santarém. (n.d.). VisitPortugal. https://www.visitportugal.com/en/NR/exeres/C24F58E7-A328-4406-BB9C-4AD3649DF85B

Igreja de São Francisco. (n.d.). Civitatis Porto. https://www.introducingporto.com/igreja-sao-francisco

Igreja de São Francisco Guimaraes. (n.d.). Nomads Travel Guide. https://www.nomads-travel-guide.com/places/igreja-de-sao-francisco-guimaraes

Igreja de São Miguel do Castelo - Guimarães. (n.d.). VisitPortugal. https://www.visitportugal.com/en/node/135228

Ilse. (2024, February 29). *20 best restaurants in Madeira – the ultimate guide*. Digital Travel Couple. https://digitaltravelcouple.com/best-restaurants-in-madeira

Is Portugal safe for travel in 2024? (2023, September 19). ViaHero. https://www.viahero.com/travel-to-portugal/is-portugal-safe

Ivanescu, Y. (2024, January 15). *Portugal packing list: Everything you need to bring in 2024*. Now in Portugal. https://nowinportugal.com/portugal-packing-list

janecanapini. (2016, November 4). *Braga, Portugal Part 2: Pilgrims, pack comfy shoes for Bom Jesus*. Grownup Travels. https://www.grownuptravels.com/bom-jesus-braga-portugal

Jardins do Palácio de Cristal. (n.d.). Civitatis Porto. https://www.introducingporto.com/jardins-do-palacio-de-cristal

Jerónimos Monastery. (n.d.). Civitatis Lisbon. https://www.lisbon.net/jeronimos-monastery

jirwin. (2020, December 20). *Cinemateca Portuguesa* (patricialotterman, Ed.). Atlas Obscura. https://www.atlasobscura.com/places/cinemateca-portuguesa

Jurga. (2023, December 13). *Faro, Portugal: 14 best things to do and places to visit (+maps and tips)*. Full Suitcase. https://fullsuitcase.com/faro-portugal

Jurga. (2024, February 23). *21 amazing things to do in Funchal, Madeira (ultimate guide)*. Full Suitcase. https://fullsuitcase.com/funchal-things-to-do

Lamberg, E. (2023, June 21). *Everything you need to know about travel insurance before you book your next trip*. CNBC. https://www.cnbc.com/select/travel-insurance-guide

Laura. (2023, September 24). *Things to do in Cascais Portugal – Europe's Fairytale Destination*. Live Adventure Travel. https://liveadventuretravel.com/things-to-do-in-cascais

Lisbon Botanical Garden. (n.d.). Museu Nacional de História Natural E Da Ciência. https://www.museus.ulisboa.pt/jardim-botanico-de-lisboa

Lisbon card: 24, 48, or 72-hour pass. (n.d.). GetYourGuide. https://www.getyourguide.com/lisbon-l42/lisboa-card-24h-48h-72h-t225711/?ranking_uuid=a6c697f0-4c1b-4c6c-9e6c-121c2b1a55e9

Lisbon Story Guesthouse. (n.d.). Booking.com. https://www.booking.com/hotel/pt/lisbon-story-guesthouse.en-gb.html

Local buses in Porto. (n.d.). Civitatis Porto. https://www.introducingporto.com/bus

Lussiana, M. (2022, January 18). *The best hotels in Guimares, Portugal for every traveler*. Culture Trip. https://theculturetrip.com/europe/portugal/articles/the-10-best-hotels-in-guimaraes

LX51 Studios & Suites by APT IIN. (n.d.). Booking.com. https://www.booking.com/hotel/pt/apt-in-lisbon-lx-51-apartments-amp-suites-lisboa12.en-gb.html

Madeira Wine Festival. (n.d.). Madeira. https://visitmadeira.com/en/whats-on/events/wine-festival

Madragoa. (n.d.). Lisbon Portugal Tourism Guide. https://www.lisbonportugaltourism.com/guide/madragoa.html

Masa Hotel 5 de Outubro. (n.d.). Booking.com. https://www.booking.com/hotel/pt/masa-5-de-outubro.en-gb.html

Meeuwesen, J. (2020, January 26). *15 best things to do in Cascais (Portugal)*. The Crazy Tourist. https://www.thecrazytourist.com/15-best-things-cascais-portugal

Memmo Alfama - Design Hotels. (n.d.). Booking.com. https://www.booking.com/hotel/pt/memmo-alfama.en-gb.html

Menu. (n.d.). A Cultura Do Hambúrguer. https://www.aculturadohamburguer.pt/menu-en.html

Michele. (2017, August 15). *Feast of the Assumption of Mary*. Algarve Housing. https://algarvehousing.net/news/feast-assumption-mary

Miller, A. (2024, April 8). *Where to stay in the Algarve Region of Portugal: Best places to stay*. WhereToStayIn.City. https://wheretostayin.city/best-places-to-stay-in-algarve

Monumentos. (n.d.). Paço Dos Duques. https://pacodosduques.pt/monumentos

Mouzinho 160. (n.d.). Booking.com. https://www.booking.com/hotel/pt/mouzinho-160-by-oporto-tourist-apartments.en.html

Museu Condes de Castro Guimarães. (n.d.). Cascais. https://www.visitcascais.com/en/resource/museu-condes-de-castro-guimaraes

Museu dos Biscaínhos. (n.d.). VisitPortugal. https://www.visitportugal.com/en/content/museu-dos-biscainhos

Museum of Fado. (n.d.). Turismo de Lisboa. https://www.visitlisboa.com/en/places/museum-of-fado

National Coach Museum. (n.d.-a). Civitatis Lisbon. https://www.lisbon.net/national-coach-museum

National Coach Museum. (n.d.-b). Turismo de Lisboa. https://www.visitlisboa.com/en/places/national-coach-museum

Nine things to do in Cascais, Portugal. (n.d.). Salt in Our Hair. https://www.saltinourhair.com/portugal/cascais-portugal

Ó Balcão. (n.d.). Michelin Guide. https://guide.michelin.com/en/santarem-region/santarm/restaurant/o-balcao

O Pizzas de Santarém. (n.d.). TheFork. https://www.thefork.com/restaurant/o-pizzas-de-santarem-r666545#tabSwitch=true

O'Brien, C. (2023, July 19). *Undiscovered Portugal: 11 hidden gems worth going to*. Live the World. https://www.livetheworld.com/post/undiscovered-portugal

On the top of the Algarve. (2021, May). Cultourista. https://www.cultourista.com/magazine/viewpoint-foia-monchique-algarve

Our menu. (n.d.). Baía Do Peixe. https://www.baiadopeixe.com/cascais

Paço dos Duques de Bragança. (n.d.). VisitPortugal. https://www.visitportugal.com/en/node/138306

Palácio da Bolsa. (2023, May 31). Portugal.com. https://www.portugal.com/location/palacio-da-bolsa

Parker, S. (2023, March 28). *Lisbon to Sintra by train: Step-by-step guide*. Big World Small Pockets. https://www.bigworldsmallpockets.com/lisbon-to-sintra-by-train

Pedras Salgadas Spa & Nature Park. (n.d.). Booking.com. https://www.booking.com/hotel/pt/pedras-salgadas-spa-and-nature-park.en-gb.html

Pedrosa, C. (2024, January 8). *The history and secrets of Livaria Lello & Irmão in Porto*. LivingTours. https://www.livingtours.com/en/blog/history-secrets-lello-bookstore-porto.html

Pensão Amor Madam's Lodge. (n.d.). Booking.com. https://www.booking.com/hotel/pt/pensao-amor-madame-39-s-lodge.en-gb.html

Petersen, B. (2023, August 3). *Garden of Santa Barbara, Braga, Portugal*. Destination Eat Drink. https://destinationeatdrink.com/garden-of-santa-barbara-braga-portugal

Pico Island: Full day wine culture tour. (n.d.). Get Your Guide. https://www.getyourguide.com/sao-miguel-island-l1663/azores-wine-tasting-tour-on-pico-island-t396568/?ranking_uuid=840f8625-357e-4f24-b25c-6c553c80e7ba

Pico Restaurant. (n.d.). Azores Wine Company. https://www.antoniomacanita.com/wineries/azores-wine-company/wine-tourism-azores/restaurant

Ponta Do Sol Inn. (n.d.). Booking.com. https://www.booking.com/hotel/pt/estalagem-da-ponta-do-sol.pt-pt.html

Portas do Sol. (n.d.). VisitPortugal. https://www.visitportugal.com/en/NR/exeres/AE0AC9FE-9EE9-4F9A-9D9F-3A1359CE4C38

Porto. (n.d.). Civitatis Porto. https://www.introducingporto.com

Porto Alegria Garden. (n.d.). Booking.com. https://www.booking.com/hotel/pt/allegra-apartment.en.html

Porto Cathedral – Sé do Porto. (n.d.). Civitatis Porto. https://www.introducingporto.com/porto-cathedral

Porto's downtown area. (n.d.). Guiajando Oporto. https://porto.travel/porto-city-centre/#Porto_downtown_A_Baixa

Portugal Bike Tours. (n.d.). Top Bike Tours Portugal. https://topbiketoursportugal.com

Portugal Homes. (2024, January 18). *Portugal travel: How to get around Portugal?* https://www.portugalhomes.com/news/article/372/portugal-travel-how-to-get-around-portugal

Portugal international travel information. (n.d.). Travel.State.gov. https://travel.state.gov/content/travel/en/international-travel/International-Travel-Country-Information-Pages/Portugal.html

Portuguese currency. (n.d.). Wise. https://wise.com/gb/travel-money/portuguese-currency

Pousada Mosteiro de Guimaraes. (n.d.). Booking.com. https://www.booking.com/hotel/pt/pousada-santa-marinha.en-gb.html

PR7.1 AVV – Caminhos do Pão e Caminhos da Fé. (n.d.). AllTrails. https://www.alltrails.com/trail/portugal/viana-do-castelo/pr7-1-avv-caminhos-do-pao-e-caminhos-da-fe

Praça do Comércio (Commerce Square). (n.d.). Civitatis Lisbon. https://www.lisbon.net/commerce-square

Restaurante Refeitro da Baixa. (n.d.). Restaurant Guru. https://restaurantguru.com/Refeitro-da-Baixa-Coimbra

Restaurante Retrokitchen. (n.d.). Restaurant Guru. https://restaurantguru.com/Retrokitchen-Braga

Retrokitchen. (n.d.). Taste Braga. https://tastebraga.com/en/restaurantes/retrokitchen-2

Ria Formosa Natural Park. (n.d.). Algarve Guide. https://www.algarvetouristguide.com/attractions/ria-formosa

Riobom, S. (2020, March 2). *What not to do in Porto and how to do instead.* Portoalities. https://portoalities.com/en/what-not-to-do-in-porto

Riobom, S. (2023, October 9). *Romantic things to do in Porto: A local's ideas.* Portoalities. https://portoalities.com/en/top-9-romantic-things-to-do-in-porto/

Rochavau Hotel. (n.d.). Booking.com. https://www.booking.com/hotel/pt/rochavau.en-gb.html

Rua Ferreira Borges (Ferreira Borges Street), Coimbra. (n.d.). GPSmyCity. https://www.gpsmycity.com/attractions/rua-ferreira-borges-(ferreira-borges-street)-45427.html

Sandeman Wine Cellar. (n.d.). Nomads Travel Guide. https://www.nomads-travel-guide.com/places/sandeman-wine-cellar

Santa Barbara Garden. (n.d.). Travel in Portugal. https://www.travel-in-portugal.com/attractions/santa-barbara-garden.htm

Santa Clara Aqueduct. (n.d.). Portugal with Kids. https://portugalwithkids.pt/en/place/santa-clara-aqueduct

Santa Marta Lighthouse Museum. (n.d.). Turismo de Lisboa. https://www.visitlisboa.com/en/places/santa-marta-lighthouse-museum

Santarem Hotel. (n.d.). Booking.com. https://www.booking.com/hotel/pt/santarem-santarem.pt-pt.html

Santarém, the belvedere city of Ribatejo | www.visitportugal.com. (n.d.). VisitPortugal. https://www.visitportugal.com/en/destinos/alentejo/73798

Santos. (n.d.). Lisbon Portugal Tourism Guide. https://www.lisbonportugaltourism.com/guide/santos.html

Santos, B. G. (2022, December 28). *Kings' Day in Portugal.* The Portugal News. https://www.theportugalnews.com/news/2022-12-28/kings-day-in-portugal/73294

Santos, N. (2018a, June 25). *10 things to know about the Santo Antonio Festival, Lisbon, Portugal.* Culture Trip. https://theculturetrip.com/europe/portugal/articles/10-things-to-know-about-the-santo-antonio-festival-lisbon-portugal

Santos, N. (2018b, July 2). *Lisbon's 8 underrated neighborhoods you should explore.* Culture Trip. https://theculturetrip.com/europe/portugal/articles/lisbons-8-underrated-neighborhoods-you-should-explore

Santuário do Bom Jesus do Monte. (n.d.). VisitPortugal. https://www.visitportugal.com/en/node/137245

São Bento Station in Porto. (n.d.). Guiajando Oporto. https://porto.travel/porto-train-station-sao-bento

São Jorge Castle. (n.d.). Civitatis Lisbon. https://www.lisbon.net/sao-jorge-castle

São Miguel: Volcano of 7 Cities crater buggy or quad tour. (n.d.). Get Your Guide. https://www.getyourguide.com/azores-l152/exploring-a-volcano-crater-quad-and-buggy-4x4-experience-t494252/?ranking_uuid=840f8625-357e-4f24-b25c-6c553c80e7ba

Schedules and prices. (n.d.). Igreja de São Francisco. https://igrejadesaofrancisco.pt/igreja/horarios

Scroope, C. (2018). *Etiquette.* Cultural Atlas. https://culturalatlas.sbs.com.au/portuguese-culture/portuguese-culture-etiquette

Sé de Faro: the Cathedral of Faro. (n.d.). AlgarveTips. https://www.algarvetips.com/cities/faro/cathedral-of-faro

Sé Velha de Coimbra. (n.d.). VisitPortugal. https://www.visitportugal.com/en/content/se-velha-coimbra

Sete Cidades (São Miguel). (n.d.). U.S. News Travel. https://travel.usnews.com/The_Azores_Portugal/Things_To_Do/Sete_Cidades_Sao_Miguel_64977/

Silva, L. (2023, May 23). *Portuguese architecture: 7 most incredible buildings in Portugal.* Portugal.com. https://www.portugal.com/history-and-culture/portuguese-architecture-7-most-incredible-buildings-in-portugal

Slavi. (2023, January 23). *What not to do in Lisbon.* Global Castaway. https://globalcastaway.com/what-not-to-do-in-lisbon

St. Louis, R. (2022, June 15). *How to get around the Algarve by car, train, boat and bicycle.* Lonely Planet. https://www.lonelyplanet.com/articles/getting-around-algarve

St. Louis, R. (2024a, February 25). *14 things Portugal locals want you to know before you visit.* Lonely Planet. https://www.lonelyplanet.com/articles/things-to-know-before-traveling-to-portugal

St. Louis, R. (2024b, March 15). *Explore the best of Porto in these top 5 neighborhoods.* Lonely Planet. https://www.lonelyplanet.com/articles/best-neighborhoods-in-porto

Stock Exchange Palace. (n.d.). Civitatis Porto. https://www.tudosobreporto.com/palacio-bolsa

Sunde-Brown, D. (n.d.-a). *Where to eat in Guimarães: The best restaurants and taverns.* Olá Daniela. https://oladaniela.com/where-to-eat-best-restaurants-guimaraes

Sunde-Brown, D. (n.d.-b). *Where to eat in the Algarve.* Olá Daniela. https://oladaniela.com/where-to-eat-in-the-algarve

Sunde-Brown, D. (2021, December 7). *6 scenic coastal drives to experience in Portugal.* The Real Word. https://www.trafalgar.com/real-word/most-scenic-coastal-drives-portugal

Sunde-Brown, D. (2024, January 7). *Where to eat in Coimbra.* Olá Daniela. https://oladaniela.com/where-to-eat-coimbra-best-restaurants

Taberna Zé-Zé. (n.d.). TheFork. https://www.thefork.com/restaurant/taberna-ze-ze-r364169

Tasquinha do Tio Júlio. (n.d.). Restaurant Guru. https://restaurantguru.com/Tio-Julio-Guimaraes-2

Taxis and Uber in Lisbon. (n.d.). Lisbon Portugal Tourism Guide. https://www.lisbonportugaltourism.com/transportation/taxis.html

Ten best seafood restaurants in the Algarve Golden Triangle. (n.d.). Unique Luxury Holidays. https://www.uniqueluxuryholidays.com/blog/10-best-seafood-restaurants-in-the-algarve-golden-triangle

The 7 most secret beaches in the Algarve. (n.d.). Portugal Collection. https://www.portugalcollection.pt/algarve-travel-guide/secret-beaches-in-the-algarve

The 10 most beautiful restaurants in Lisbon. (n.d.). Lisbon Lux. https://www.lisbonlux.com/magazine/the-10-most-beautiful-restaurants-in-lisbon

The 10 most romantic things to do in Lisbon. (n.d.). Lisbon Lux. https://www.lisbonlux.com/magazine/romantic-lisbon-sunsets-and-fairytales

The Arch – charming apartments in the historic center. (n.d.). Booking.com. https://www.booking.com/hotel/pt/the-arch-charming-apartments-in-the-historic-center.fr.html

The Church of St. Francis, Porto. (2024, March 12). Portugal.com. https://www.portugal.com/location/the-church-of-st-francis-porto

The Crystal Palace. (n.d.). Guiajando Oporto. https://porto.travel/palacio-de-cristal

The Editors of Encyclopaedia Britannica. (n.d.-a). Azores. In *Encyclopedia Britannica.* Retrieved April 10, 2024, from https://www.britannica.com/place/Azores

The Editors of Encyclopaedia Britannica. (n.d.-b). Braga. In *Encyclopedia Britannica.* Retrieved April 4, 2024, from https://www.britannica.com/place/Braga-city-Portugal

The Editors of Encyclopaedia Britannica. (n.d.-c). Faro. In *Encyclopedia Britannica.* Retrieved April 12, 2024, from https://www.britannica.com/place/Faro-Portugal

The Editors of Encyclopaedia Britannica. (n.d.-d). Guimarães. In *Encyclopedia Britannica.* Retrieved April 12, 2024, from https://www.britannica.com/place/Guimaraes

The Editors of Encyclopaedia Britannica. (n.d.-e). Madeira Islands. In *Encyclopædia Britannica.* Retrieved April 10, 2024, from https://www.britannica.com/place/Madeira-Islands

The Editors of Encyclopaedia Britannica. (n.d.-f). Santarém. In *Encyclopedia Britannica.* Retrieved April 12, 2024, from https://www.britannica.com/place/Santarem-Portugal

The essential guide to Ria Formosa Natural Park. (n.d.). Formosamar. https://formosamar.com/the-essential-guide-to-ria-formosa

The Foundation history. (n.d.). Serralves. https://www.serralves.pt/en/institucional-serralves/1.5.-_ok-fundacao---historia

The history of the oldest town in Portugal. (n.d.). Museu Pio XII. https://www.museupioxii.pt/en

The House of Sandeman – Hostel & Suites. (n.d.). Booking.com. https://www.booking.com/hotel/pt/the-house-of-sandeman-hostel-suites.en.html

The Lodge Hotel. (n.d.). Booking.com. https://www.booking.com/hotel/pt/the-lodge-wine-amp-business.en.html

The menu. (n.d.). Santa Maria Hostel + Restaurante. https://www.santamariafunchal.com/restaurant

The museum. (n.d.). Museu Dos Biscainhos. https://museudosbiscainhos.gov.pt/museu

The Old Cathedral of Coimbra (Sé Velha de Coimbra). (n.d.). Ulysses Travel. https://www.ulysses.travel/en/old-cathedral-of-coimbra-se-velha-de-coimbra

The Vine Hotel. (n.d.). Booking.com. https://www.booking.com/hotel/pt/the-vine.en-gb.html

Three Marias Guest House B&B. (n.d.). Booking.com. https://www.booking.com/hotel/pt/3-marias-guest-house.fr.html

Ticket office. (n.d.). Torre Dos Clérigos. https://www.torredosclerigos.pt/en/ticket-office

Time Out Porto Editors. (2023, September 8). *The 21 best restaurants in Porto.* TimeOut. https://www.timeout.com/porto/restaurants/the-best-porto-restaurants

Tips for visiting the Algarve. (2022, August 8). A Portuguese Affair. https://www.aportugueseaffair.com/tips-for-visiting-the-algarve

Top 10 must-see attractions in Coimbra. (n.d.). Coimbra Portugal Tourism Guide. https://www.coimbraportugaltourism.com/guide/top-10-things-to-see-and-do-in-coimbra.html

Top 10 things to do in Baixa. (2017, June 28). TimeOut. https://www.timeout.com/porto/things-to-do/top-10-things-to-do-in-baixa

Torre dos Clérigos. (n.d.). Visit Portugal. https://www.visitportugal.com/en/content/torre-dos-clerigos

Tourism. (n.d.). Associacão Comercial Do Porto. https://palaciodabolsa.com/en/tourism

Travelling by local bus in Porto. (n.d.). Local Porto. https://www.localporto.com/travelling-by-bus-porto

Travelling by metro in Porto. (n.d.). Local Porto. https://www.localporto.com/travelling-by-metro-in-porto

Twenty-eight best things to do in Braga, Portugal. (2023, November 19). Jetsetting Fools. https://jetsettingfools.com/things-to-do-in-braga-portugal

Universidade de Coimbra. (n.d.). VisitPortugal. https://www.visitportugal.com/en/NR/exeres/212BDD2D-3DC6-4836-BCD7-BBB9011C5036

Vargas, R. (2024, September 1). *Culture and social etiquette in Portugal.* Expatica. https://www.expatica.com/pt/living/integration/etiquette-in-portugal-106561/#regional

ViajePortugal. (n.d.-a). *Bairrada Winery Route Experience, full-day from Coimbra.* Tripadvisor. https://www.tripadvisor.ca/AttractionProductReview-g189143-d19874102-Bairrada_Winery_Route_Experience_full_day_from_Coimbra-Coimbra_Coimbra_District_Ce.html

ViajePortugal. (n.d.-b). *Best Flavors of Bairrada Winery Route, half day from Coimbra.* Tripadvisor. https://www.tripadvisor.ca/AttractionProductReview-g189143-d15534404-Best_Flavors_of_Bairrada_Winery_Route_half_day_from_Coimbra-Coimbra_Coimbra_Distri.html

Vila Nova de Gaia – Portugal holiday guide. (n.d.). Travel in Portugal. https://www.travel-in-portugal.com/vila-nova-de-gaia

Visit. (n.d.-a). Museu Nacional Dos Coches. http://museudoscoches.gov.pt/pt/visite

Visit. (n.d.-b). Serralves. https://www.serralves.pt/visitar-serralves

Visit and tastings. (n.d.). Graham's Port. https://grahams-port.com/visits-tastings

Visit the Museum, feel the Fado and visit the exhibitions. (n.d.). Museu Do Fado. https://www.museudofado.pt/en/visit

Visit us. (n.d.). Sandeman Port Wine Cellars. https://www.sandeman.com/port-wine/visit/cellars-porto

Vó Bela. (n.d.). TheFork. https://www.thefork.com/restaurant/vo-bela-r814117

Where to watch the sunset in the Algarve. (n.d.). Baía Da Luz. https://www.baiadaluz.com/en/where-to-watch-the-sunset-in-the-algarve

Wine Tourism in Portugal. (2021, July 19). *10 wineries you can't miss in Douro.* https://blog.winetourismportugal.com/10-wineries-you-cant-miss-in-douro

Made in United States
North Haven, CT
11 November 2024

60128912R00085